Beat Inflation
Protect Savings

Authored by:
Louis Rubin

Researched by the staff of:
Wealth Achievers, Inc.

List of Advisories

Advisory 1

The True Cost of Inflation

There are four prime reasons you must learn to invest:

1. To put inflation to work for you.

2. To increase your income.

3. To make your capital grow.

4. To learn to turn your tax liabilities into assets.

In this chapter we'll take an unemotional look at inflation and the devastating path it has cut across the face of the United States, bringing havoc to many a financial plan.

Inflation, the Robin Hood of the 1980's

Inflation was the Robin Hood of the 1970's and will continue to be the Super Robin Hood of the 1980's. Through the efforts of the Reagan administration, its rate of growth can decrease, but the direction is still upward even at a decreasing rate. Nin percent inflation is admittedly better than 15 percent, but even at that rate our cost of living will double in eight years.

Accept this fact of life and make your decisions about money accordingly. If I can leave only one thought with you, after you have read this book, it is this: deal with life as it truly is and not the way you wish it were. This chapter will give you the facts about inflation. This book will enlighten you as to ways that can make inflation work for you rather than against you. There is probably nothing in your economic life that can make as much money for you as inflation if you understand how it works, learn to embrace it rather than fear it, and harness its energy.

Inflation does not destroy wealth. It does not reduce the number of houses that builders can build, the amount of wheat that farmers can produce, or the number of telephones that Ma Bell can install. Inflation redistributes wealth. It takes it from those who do not understand how it works and gives it to those who do.

Inflation takes from the ignorant and gives to the well informed. You will be either its victim or its beneficiary. It will make you a winner or a loser. The choice is yours. It's much more fun being a winner. All you need to do is recognize that inflation is a fact of your life-an economic force in the world or suffer its dire consequences. Inflation has been your constant companion since the day you were born, and from all indications it will continue to be with you for the remainder of your life. This problem does not exist in the United States alone, but has been felt worldwide. Tolstoy chronicled that every civilized nation that has ever existed has experienced the ravages of inflation.

Poor Richard Hits the Fan

During the dust bowl of Oklahoma there was a Puritan ethic embodied in *Poor Richard's Almanac*-"Work Hard, Be Thrifty, don't borrow."

Were you raised under Poor Richard's Guidelines? If you were, throw off his shackles this very minute. He'll drag you down to the bottom of inflation's ocean, and you won't surface in time for resuscitation.

Have you been exposed for years to the "Prudent Man's Rule," so dear to the hearts of regulatory agencies that decide whether you have prudently managed pension funds under your trusteeship or other fiduciary responsibilities? If you have, and have faithfully followed the old guidelines of 40 percent in corporate bonds and the remainder in very, very blue chip common stocks, you and the beneficiaries of your pension plan have been losers and from all indications will continue to be losers. With the continuing battering of inflation, the "Prudent Man's Rule" has now become the "Stupid Man's Rule."

You will find the "Poor Richard" and 'Prudent Man's" philosophy very hard to escape, for it is all around you. Today as you drive down the freeway to work, strategically positioned at a curve in the road, in brilliant lights, you may see a billboard emblazoned in bold print that reads:

"INVEST IN SERIES E BONDS TO GAURANTEE

YOUR FUTURE"

Is this false advertising? Can you name a ten-year period in the past thirty years when investing in a Series E bond has "guaranteed your future?" Can you name even one year in the past decade when, after inflation (and later after taxes), your money maintained the only value worth maintaining-its purchasing power?

I read about an interview recently in which the U.S. Savings Bonds people were asked, "Does it pay to save when the inflation rates have been exceeding the rates on Savings Bonds?" And the added question was put to them, "Under these circumstances can you really say you are saving?"

The Savings Bond spokesman's reply was, "Yes, for if you didn't save, you'd be that much further behind." It would appear that he was conceding that a loss was involved, but he insisted a loss could be a gain.

If it doesn't pay to save, you might be asking, does it pay to spend? Often it does, if you have exchanged your paper money for something more durable that has an opportunity to retain its value-in other words, if you have moved your money out of paper and into things. Once you have brought yourself to making this decision, you have opened yourself to a wide range of other decisions: Which things? When? At what price? At what location? This book should give you some of the answers.

You live in a world of change. Every day is a new day. Financial survival requires the best use of your intelligence, experience, agility, continuous study, daily diligence, and discipline. But your rewards can be so great that the investment of your time and energy in this endeavor can make it all worthwhile. There will be times, if you are not always on guard, when you may be lulled into a false sense of security, and you'll temporarily let down your defenses. You may hear one of the government's "inflation fighters" make an optimistic announcement, or you may have received something comparable to the big WIN button we were given back in the Ford administration to wear, but don't be deceived. Inflation will continue. (In case you've forgotten, WIN stood for Whip Inflation Now.)

What Causes Inflation?

Your government itself is the chief cause of inflation. It does this not by trying to give you what you hate, but by trying to give you the goodies you want-such as full employment, health insurance that you won't buy for yourself, "entitlement," a word that has been bandied around in recent years. Many politicians equate entitlement to being "entitled to" support from the cradle to the grave, often without any relationship to effort on the part of the recipient, just because they were fortunate enough to have been born in the United States.

If our forefathers were writing the Bill of Rights today, after having lived in our environment for a number of years, they would add a clause to their bill saying that every person is entitled to a job. Before World War II this was not a commonly held belief. Before then, prices went up, but they also went down, so prices remained essentially stable. Now that so many believe in their right to job security and are abetted by the philosophy of a host of congressional members that you can solve any problem if you just cover it with it enough appropriations, inflation has gone on a rampage, not only here but abroad, for we have exported this concept.

The year after World War II, Congress passed the 'full employment act," which declared that our government would vigorously promote both price and stability and full employment. Even a college freshman with no more exposure to economics than Economics 101 should know that those two are inconsistent goals.

The employment Act of 1946 was to be the embodiment of utopia, and brilliant government administrators would do a balancing act whereby high employment rates could be generated by accepting higher inflation. But what has the implementation of this theory wrought? We have found that employment that results from inflation lasts for only a short period of time, and in order to restimulate employment, inflation must again be accelerated. Always remember that full employment brings the politicians more votes than does licking inflation; therefore the majority of politicians will opt for full employment.

Inflation also makes it easier to meet any economic crises that may occur. For example, look at what happened to Penn Central and Franklin National Bank. There was a time when bankruptcies, like unemployment, were a natural phenomena. Today, Washington abhors such occurrences, so it lends money to Lockheed, becomes Franklin National Bank's low-cost supplier of funds, and guarantees Chrysler's loans and New York City's bonds.

It is incongruous that a government of what is billed as a capitalistic free-enterprise system took badly needed capital from other areas of our economy and subsidized Chrysler, one of our worst-managed companies. This was done in the name of preservation of jobs, when that same amount of money put to work in more efficient areas would have created more jobs. To add to this unbelievable situation, the support came at a time when one of the most efficiently run industries, the oil industry, was being criticized and penalized for making profits. When we reward the inefficient and penalize the efficient, we increase inflation by disrupting the natural balance of supply and demand. We also put more pressure on the government to deficit-spend and these deficits lead directly to more inflation.

Dilution

If you learn to substitute the word *dilution* every time you see the word *inflation*, you will come to have a better understanding of inflation. As Congress votes to expand currency and credit to finance bail-outs of the automobile industry, the housing industry, and welfare, it in turn dilutes the purchasing power of your money. As you can readily see, if another million dollars of currency were to be printed and circulated for every million already in circulation, twice as many dollars would be chasing the same amount of goods and services, so they would rise to twice their original price. The true value of goods and services has not risen. The value of currency has been cut in half by doubling its quantity-hence dilutions have occurred.

A more graphic way of looking at the effect of inflation is to look at a dollar composed of quarters that you have held since 1900. Youi now go to the grocery store to make a purchase. How much do you think your dollar will buy in the form of goods and services in comparison with what it bought in 1900? Your dollar has lost 92 percent of the only value it has-what it will buy. A dollar has no value in and of itself. Its only value is what you can exchange it for in the marketplace. What you want to store for the future is not so many dollars, but so many pairs of shoes, tubes of lipstick, and hamburgers. In 1940, you could go to your local grocery store and buy ten loaves of bread for $1. By 1950, you could buy only four, by 1970 only three, and by 1980 only one. How many will your dollar buy today? It is the same dollar, but it has lost the major portion of its only value.

If I can do nothing else for you in this book but help you to convert your thinking from dollars to bread, I will have done you an immense favor. I warn you, it is an emotional transition that only a few can make. If you can make it, you will be in the minority-but remember, it's only the minority that become financially independent.

Between 1940 and 1979, the dollar held its own in only two years, and then by less than 1 percent. Not even a professional gambler would accept those odds. Yet, if you are holding a dollar today, you are betting against those odds. If you are a saver, placing your savings in a "guaranteed" position, you are a gambler, and if the past is any indication of the future, you are "guaranteed" to lose!

What if I were to say to you, "I want to recommend a stock for your serious consideration. I know that its record has not been very good, but I have faith that it will approve. It was selling for $100 in 1952; by 1957 it had dropped to $96; by 1962 to $88; by 1967 to $79; by 1972 to $63; and by 1977 it was $44. Today it is at $28, but don't let that discourage you. I still have faith in this investment, and I want you to invest in it." If I were to make such a "buy" recommendation to you, what would you say to me? Before you say, "You've got to be kidding!" I want you to know that this investment is recommended by most of our states and national banks, by all of our savings and loan companies, by all of the nation's life insurance companies that sell cash surrender value policies, by your city, and by the federal government itself. What is this investment? It is the U.S. dollar!

It Is the U.S. Dollar

"Guaranteed" dollars are recommended as a good, "safe" investment for you by all savings institutions and insurance companies that sell cash surrender value life insurance; yet they never want a "guaranteed" dollar for themselves. They want to "guarantee" your principal, "guarantee" your rate of return, and "guarantee" that y our dollar will for them-usually harder than it works for you. You will receive a "guarantee" that you can always get back each deflating dollar you have placed with them (excluding "your" savings account with the life insurance company). You are also guaranteed that you will never receive any more than that dollar, plus compound interest you may have left with them, regardless of what the cost of living has become.

The Tax Bracket Creeper

There is a hideous monster lurking in the Internal Revenue Service tax rate schedule that you may not be aware of that can bring devastation to your financial planning. It's not the "Cookie Monster"; it is the "Bracket Creeper Monster." The monster hides out in the fine print of the IRS tax schedule, and it feeds especially on inflation. In the past ten years, the prices you have had to pay for your daily living expenses have doubled, but you may not think they are affecting you because you've been receiving cost-of-living raises to help you maintain your purchasing power. What you have failed to notice is the "Bracket Creeper Monster." Your higher income has pushed you into a higher tax bracket. For example, if your taxable income was $20,000 mand you filed a joint return ten years ago, you paid $4,380 in federal income taxes, and had $15,620 left after taxes to enable you to keep pace with inflation. Your employer has by now raised your salary until your taxable income is $40,000, making you owe a federal income tax of $9,195 and leaving you $30,805 after taxes. But to keep even, you would need $61,610. Your federal income taxes increased 110 percent while your cost of living increased 100 percent.

The average working couple earning $35,200 a year will pay more than one-third of their income in taxes. On a national level, federal and state income taxes after all exemptions and deductions will average 11.6 percent of personal income; but other taxes such as sales, excise, customs, property, Social Security, and franchise more than triple the bite.

Taxes have risen a massive 46 percent as share of personal income in the past three decades. Americans today are taxed 26 cents for every dollar earned. Social Security is our fastest rising federal tax.

The Reagan tax "cut" under ERTA cut the rate of taxation for the first time since the Kennedy administration. This does not mean that the average American will be taxed less' it only means that he would have paid even more without the rate reduction.

Under ERTA, indexing to the dull effect of the "Bracket Creeper Monster" it was supposed to begin in 1985. Few believe that politicians will let this happen, because it will greatly reduce their aura of magnificent largess.

U.S federal tax collections from citizens who do not take steps to protect themselves through proper planning increase an average of 16 percent for every 10 percent of increase in personal income. If you live in a state with progressive state income taxes, such as California and New York, inflation causes an increase in the state bite as well. As a result, the government has a vested interest in maintaining inflation, since our laws permit a windfall tax bonus every year we have inflation.

Poor Richard advised "don't borrow," but inflation has made his advice obsolete. Inflation rewards those who owe money, not those who pay cash. I'm not talking about plastic money-your Visa, MasterCard, or American Express cards. Never charge anything you can't pay for in thirty days. Never borrow for your daily living or luxuries. Only borrow long-term for investing-never for spending.

Let's look at the balance sheet of three families and see which family was the most prudent in an inflationary economy.

The Anderson family's balance sheet looks like this:

Cash	$10,000	Mortgage	$5,000
Home	10,000	Net worth	$15,000

Net worth is the difference between your assets and your liabilities and is a measure of how rich you are.

Now let's assume that prices double. The Andersons' balance sheet will now look like this:

Cash	$10,000	Mortgage	$5,000
Home	20,000	Net worth	25,000

The Andersons' net worth has now increased from $15,000 to $25,000, which at first glance appears good; however, their net worth has not doubled, as prices did. Therefore, this family has fallen behind in the inflation rate. Their wealth or purchasing power has been reduced by inflation.

Now let's examine the Barton family's balance sheet:

Cash	$5,000	Mortgage	$5,000
Home	10,000	Net worth	10,000

A doubling of prices has this effect on their balance sheet:

Cash	$5,000	Mortgage	$5,000
Home	20,000	Net worth	20,000

The Bartons have held their own. They have exactly kept pace with inflation.

Now let's look at the Calloway family's balance sheet:

Cash	$3,000	Mortgage	$10,000
Home	12,000	Net worth	17,000

When prices doubled the Calloway's net worth looked like this:

Cash	$3,000	Mortgage	$10,000
Home	24,000	Net worth	17,000

The Calloways' net worth increased from $5,000 to $17,000, or more than tripled, while prices only doubled. The Calloways beat inflation.

What lesson about inflation have you learned from these three families? Is it this sad commentary: "Inflation often rewards those who owe long-term debt, not those who pay cash"?

This does not mean you should overleverage. The inflation rate also fluctuates, and there will be times when it is increasing at a decreasing rate. When you receive such indications, reduce your leveraging until the trend reverses.

You don't have to be on the verge of bankruptcy to benefit from inflation. You can and should have cash, but you will want to have a large amount of your assets invested in things that can inflate with the cost of living. Again, I emphasize, own the thing that owns the thing. To win the inflation game in the years ahead, you will have to learn to use leverage wisely. Your assets must be primarily in investments that can rise as fast as the general price levels at each stage of the inflation cycle. There was a time when families did not feel comfortable unless they had cash in the bank. Today families feel uncomfortable with money in the bank. For the first time in our history, a large number of our citizens will be searching for better ways to store their future purchasing power.

Inflation Does Not Hurt the Knowledgeable

Inflation will not hurt you if you become knowledgeable and act to protect yourself from it. But you will be saddened as you look around and see the tragic faces of the hard-working, thrifty, sacrificing persons who have faithfully saved and put their money where they have been told it would be safe and have lost their money's only true value-its purchasing power. With it they have also lost the privilege of retiring in financial dignity. At least the spendthrifts had the fun of spending their money until they got off the inflation train. During their working years, their raises usually matched or exceeded their cost-of living increases. But when they got off the inflation train and it went on without them, they had no chance of keeping up with the inflationary spiral.

The Total Portfolio

To take advantage of the transfers that inflation makes in wealth, you must begin by thinking in terms of a total portfolio that you will have positioned efficiently at the proper time to beat inflation. Your portfolio must maximize your after-tax return balanced against a level of risk that provides you with peace of mind. You will want to avoid fads unless you are equipped emotionally to act rapidly. As inflation pushes up the price of your assets, faddists will start jumping in with both feet. At this point prices will begin to over discount inflation. The faddist will be selling as prices drop. You will want to be in a position to buy at that time.

To beat inflation, you will always want to be holding the right combination of assets. This means an investment for each season, but not an investment for all seasons. This means that nothing you have can be just put away in in your safe-deposit box and forgotten. You must learn to be flexible and alert.

You should classify all the investment vehicles valuable to you as to their appropriateness for accelerating inflation or decelerating inflation. Then decide whether inflation is about to accelerate or decelerate.

Many who come to me for financial counseling have already accumulated sufficient assets, or could easily do so within a few years, to enable them to reach or work toward financial independence, if these assets were properly put to work. This may be true for you. You may be working extremely hard for your money, but unfortunately once it is obtained, instead of putting it to work for yourself, you have unknowingly given away its earning power. You cannot afford to have your money working for others. If you do, you'll lose the money and the tax game!

Inflation will be a part of your life for as long as you live. You can fear it, hide your head in the sand, and say that it doesn't exist or that it will go away, but you are only kidding yourself and inviting financial disappointments. Inflation can be your valuable ally. You can use it to increase your wealth by applying your intelligence and energy to studying the inflation cycles and positioning your assets at the proper location at the proper time. You must face the reality that you will probably never own an asset that is immune to the inflation cycle.

The facing of this reality and your determination to use these forces can be a challenging and profitable undertaking.

ADVISORY 2

What Is Money?

Where do we begin?

Let's go back to the very basics, so there can be no misunderstanding between us as we proceed to the conclusions.

If you were to find yourself alone on an isolated island, you'd have no need for a medium of exchange. There would be no one with whom to exchange.

You would go to work, as necessary, to produce the things you needed for survival. You'd produce some things you would want to consume immediately, and you would probably produce other things to be stored for later use.

You might also produce some other things that would be called "capital goods"-things that make further production easier. But you would only produce when you believed it would lead ultimately to something you wanted.

Not hard to understand, is it?

Let's suppose now that there was one other person on the island with you. Each of you has his own area of the island and each of you is producing for himself.

Sooner or later, you'd probably begin exchanging things with each other. Perhaps you've produced more than you need of something he hasn't produced, and vice versa. You'd exchange your surplus with each other-and both of you would profit thereby.

Obviously, you won't trade your production for something you have no use for. Why bother working if your efforts don't eventually bring you something you can use? You'll trade only for those things you want to use now or can store for use at a later date.

And here we have a very important rule at work, one that we should file mentally for reference later on: *You only produce or exchange when you believe it will lead ultimately to something you want.*

On such a simple basis, with only one or two people involved, it's very easy to see and understand what's happening. You're producing and exchanging in order to acquire the things you'll eventually uses to further your own well-being.

But now let's suppose there are a 100 people on the island-each in his own area. You will still have to produce to survive; there's no way to avoid that.

But exchanges will probably take place on a much wider basis. In fact, it will be only a matter of time until a "specialization of labor" develops. That's where an individual no longer produces everything for himself. Instead, he concentrates on the production of only one or two items-and then trades his production with others for the products and services he wants.

You know that no one's going to exchange with you if you don't have something he wants. So you'll gear your production to those things that are in demand by others. In that way, you'll get the most possible in return.

These trades with others are called *direct exchange*-the trading of some of your property for another commodity you intend to use yourself. This is also called *barter*-trading without money.

INDIRECT EXCHANGE

But, eventually, you find yourself in a position where you're willing to accept in exchange and item you don't intend to use. You accept it only to improve your trading position with someone else.

Suppose you have butter and you're looking for wheat. I have wheat, but I'm *not* looking for butter. Instead, I need corn. So you go find a third person who has corn and is looking for butter. You trade your butter for his corn. Then you come back to me and trade the corn for my wheat.

You have what you want; but it took two exchanges to get it.

This is the beginning of *indirect exchange*-the trading of one thing for something you *don't* intend to use yourself.

For example, one-day Jones the nail-maker walks into the store of Smith the furniture-maker (whose store is conveniently located under a palm tree). Jones opens the conversation with, "Smith, I need a new workbench. I'll give 2,000 nails to make one for me.

"Sorry," said Smith, "I have all the nails I'll need for awhile. Those you gave me for the bed I made for you will last me for another six months. Come back and see me then."

Determined not to be refused, Jones goes on, "But I need the workbench now! Look, you're bound to use those nails eventually. But, even in the meantime, you can probably trade them to someone else for something you need. I'm always getting offers of trades from people wanting nails. They're a lot easier to exchange than furniture."

You have a point there," ponders Smith. "I do seem to have a lot of trouble exchanging a king size beds for cloths. This way I'd use only as many nails as I need for each purchase...well, okay-I'll try anything once."

So he accepts the nails and makes the workbench for Jones. And then he goes out to find products for which he can exchange the nails.

And, lo and behold, it works! He finds that trades are much easier to make. As a result, he enjoys life a lot more with a few nails in his pocket. He can stop at a store and trade for anything he wants to-without having to exchange a king-size bed for a peanut-butter sandwich.

In fact, he merely points out to the merchant the advantages of nails as a trading medium in the same way that Jones pointed then out to him. And the final argument is that you can always use the nails *sometime* in the future; they won't lose their value. And if *you* don't use them, *someone* will.

The merchant realizes this; and so he accepts the nails, confident that he can use them or trade them for what he wants.

In the months to follow, Jones the nail-maker notices a slow steady increase in the demand for his product. Why? Because individuals, *one at a time*, are coming to see that it's valuable to have a few extra nails on hand (in addition to those needed for construction purposes) to facilitate exchanges with others.

Nails seem to most people on the island to be the most ideal trading medium. But once there are enough nails around for that purpose, the demand will level off. The nails are not free; they cost Jones his time to make them and he demands something in return when he trades them with others. So no one's going to pay for more nails than he'll find useful to have.

As a result, once there are enough nails in circulation to facilitate exchange, there'll be no additional value from more nails. In other words, like any other commodity, they seek their natural level of quantity, their market price.

Let's go back a moment to the point we recognized on page twenty: *You only produce or exchange when you believe it will lead ultimately to something you want.*

Smith, the furniture-maker, didn't produce the workbench just for the sake of producing. In his eyes, his profit didn't come from the number of beds or workbenches produced.

Neither did his satisfaction come from the number he sold. To be able to say he sold a certain number of pieces of furniture was of no particular value to him.

To Smith, the object of it all was to obtain things he wanted. He produced and sold furniture with only one purpose in mind-to trade it for the specific things *he* wanted. So he wouldn't make a workbench just to be making a workbench. Nor would he accept nails just so he could say he'd made a sale.

He agreed to Jones's offer only when he was convinced it was a step toward getting what he wanted.

And this is a vital point. Neither production volume nor sales volume is ever the object. It's only what you eventually receive for it that counts. You only produce and exchange when you believe it will lead ultimately to something you want.

We will have occasion to come back to this seemingly obvious point as we proceed. But, meanwhile, we see that this simple little trade has been the seed from which indirect exchange is born on the island.

And it naturally grows in use and acceptance, it opens up all kinds of new possibilities for residents of the community. Now it's possible for one man to employ another, paying him with nails instead of with fractions of a house. Now long-term capital investments can be made-by trading one's production for nails, purchasing capital goods with the nails, making a new product, and finally selling it.

So nails have become money. And what is money?

Money is a commodity that is accepted in exchange by an individual who intends to trade it for something else.

Money is a commodity, just like everything else that's traded in the marketplace. What distinguishes a money commodity from other commodities is the intention of the recipient to keep it only until he trades it to someone else. It's only a means to a further exchange for that recipient.

Not *everyone* intends to trade it, however. Some people receive the money commodity, intending to use it for its own natural purpose (in this case, nails for construction purposes).

And this brings us to the key word in the definition of money: *accepted*. The commodity can become money only when an individual *accepts* it-when someone's willing to take it, confident that he can trade it ultimately for what *he* wants.

You only produce and exchange when you believe it'll lead ultimately to something you want. So you won't accept bamboo reeds-just because someone wants something you have.

The commodity to be used as money must already have established itself as being in demand-otherwise, you'd never be sure you could trade it for later for something you wanted.

Because of this, the money commodity is never chosen by a majority vote; it's never initially imposed upon a community by a government; it's never collectively nor arbitrarily selected. It *evolves-one exchange at a time*-as one individual and then another decides to accept it in exchange.

Governments can only choose to go along with what has naturally evolved in the marketplace. If they stray from that, they're doomed to destruction. For money only takes on value as individuals are willing to accept it. But we'll come back to governments later.

To summarize, the money commodity will emerge, one exchange at a time, as each individual sees the commodity, evaluates it, and agrees to accept it-believing this will further his ability to obtain eventually the item he wants.

In our island example, the individual accepted the nails because he knew how much money they were worth in terms of other commodities; and he knew that, come what may, they'd always be of some value to him. He knew he'd never be "stuck" with nails (pardon the pun) because he could also use them himself.

As we've seen, the volume of nails would be determined by the number of nails that proved useful in exchange, together with the normal demand for nails in construction. Beyond that, any additional production of nails by Jones would be worthless to him; more nails would simply lessen the exchange value of each nail. So he'd be working harder (producing more nails) but getting no more in return.

If he tried to demand more for his nails than individuals were willing to give (the market value), he be inviting competition. For someone else could then offer nails at a lower exchange price; or possibly even offer a more useful commodity as a medium of exchange.

So Jones's success will still depend upon his technical ability and marketing sense; he has no special advantage just because he's the man who produces the money commodity.

WHY GOLD AND SILVER?

It's quite possible that more than one commodity might be used as money-either in the same or in neighboring communities. The only question that matters is: will an individual be willing to accept the commodity in an exchange?

But it is only natural that consumers will begin to rely upon the one or two commodities that best satisfy their needs and desires in exchanges. Despite hundreds of different commodities that have been used as money at various times and places in history, two commodities have dominated the money markets for centuries. They are *gold* and *silver*.

But why gold and silver?

As we've seen, the development would have had to be purely natural-one exchange at a time-adding up to billions of trades. No one person or group ever decided that it would be so. But, in retrospect, we can look back and understand *why* gold and silver become supreme.

There are five main attributes of gold and silver that give individuals good reason to *accept* these commodities confidently:

1. Both commodities are *durable*. They can be stores for long periods of time, if necessary, without perishing. Obviously, bananas won't do. Imagine saving up for a new car, then going to the closet to take out your savings, only to find out they were rotten.

2. The commodities are easily *divisible*. As we saw, it was easier to exchange nails than furniture because you could divide a supply of nails into small purchases. And gold and silver can be broken into smaller pieces or used as dust-without harming their inherent value in any way.

3. Gold and silver are relatively *convenient* to handle. Their naturally high market values make it possible to work with small quantities. Paper wouldn't do-because you'd need so much of it to be worth a desired item that it would be inconvenient to carry and exchange.

4. Gold and silver are each *consistent* in quality. Once it has been assayed and its fineness determined,

one ounce of gold is as good as any other ounce of the same fineness. This simplifies exchange negotiations.

For short periods in history, each of these four rules has been violated by various commodities that still managed to serve adequately as money. But for a commodity to suffice as money, a fifth attribute is absolutely necessary. For we're talking about human beings whose futures and securities are at stake. And they won't produce and exchange unless they believe it will lead ultimately to something useful.

This means the individual must be confident that what he is receiving today will be exchangeable tomorrow. And how can he be sure of that?

5. The commodity must have *accepted value*. It must be usable ad already accepted for a non-money purpose before it can serve as money. Only then can the recipient be sure he isn't receiving a white elephant.

Gold is a commodity-just like lettuce, nails, bricks, or toothpaste. Gold has its own uses. In fact, gold and silver are used for such things as jewelry, dental work, electronics, art objects, ornamentation, soldering, photography, and other purpose. If gold weren't money, it would still circulate in the world because of its other uses. (We normally refer to the non-money uses a s *commercial* or *industrial* uses.)

So you never have to worry about gold going out of style as a money item. Its continued value is based upon something sure and reliable. If your neighbor refuses to accept it in exchange from you, you can still take it to a jeweler or a dental supply company and receive something of value for it.

That previously determined value also tells you *how much* gold is worth in relationship to other commodities.

If the money commodity didn't have that separate value, you couldn't confidently accept it in trade for what you have produced, for you wouldn't know the worth of what you received.

Gold, as either an industrial or monetary commodity, is subject to the same laws of supply and demand as is any commodity. Overproduction will cause its market value to drop.

On the other hand, a *shortage* of gold would increase its value and thereby encourage prospecting and production. There has never really been a long-term shortage of gold in the world; and there certainly isn't one today. It is being produced at an ever increasing rate.

But we're getting ahead of ourselves. The evolution of our money system must continue.

Up to this point, we've recognized two important signposts what will have great significance when we get to the practical application of these principles of money:

1. You only produce or exchange when you believe it will lead ultimately to something you want.

2. Money is a commodity that is accepted in exchange by an individual who intends to trade it for something else.

Putting these two together, we find that you would not accept "money" in exchange if you didn't believe it would lead to the purchase of an item you really wanted.

That leads us to some further developments in money. In the next few pages, we'll see the transition from the primitive society (our island example, employed to isolate the purpose of each individual in an exchange) to the modern, complicated economy in which we live.

WHAT IS PAPER?

In any market, the natural impulse of an ambitious individual is to look around for ways of making life easier for other people-knowing they will pay him a handsome profit for what he makes available to them.

Now that our little community has grown, and gold has replaced nails as the major money commodity, one enterprising fellow notices that individuals waste a lot of time measuring gold dust in exchange for their drinks at the bar.

So he opens a mint. He buys raw gold or silver from miners and converts the metal into coins. He stamps the coins with his name and the amount of gold inside the coin.

If an individual trusts the coin-maker, he will probably prefer to use the coin in exchange. Its recognizable weight makes it easier than measuring gold dust.

But since no one wants to trade for something that may be worthless, he must be sure there's really gold (in the amount indicated) inside the coin. Not only that, he has to know that others will accept the coin, too.

The coins must be stamped with the seal of someone who has gained widespread respect in the marketplace. For an individual will be willing to accept the coin only when he's sure of the value in the commodity in the coin.*

Exchange is easier as individuals trade coins instead of continually measuring gold dust.

* In case you're wondering if this applies to copper-nickel "coins," we will come to them shortly.

But the evolution continues. Another ambitious chap opens a warehouse. "Bring your gold to me," he says. "I'll store it for you in a theft-proof vault. I'll give you a receipt for your gold, so you can claim it any time you want it. I only charge a small fee for the service of storing it for you."

This means you can now keep your gold in a safe warehouse-rather than having it at home where it could be stolen.

You have the receipts in your possession; you can take them to the warehouse and get your gold whenever you need it.

And as the use of the warehouse becomes more wide spread, and the integrity of the warehouseman becomes known, the receipts can serve an additional purpose. You can exchange the receipts themselves.

Why bother going to the warehouse to get your gold, only to trade it to someone who will probably take it back to the same warehouse for safekeeping? Instead, you simply hand over the receipt to him. In the process, title to the gold has passed from you to him.

Receipts add to the ease of exchange because it's easier to transfer the paper than the gold itself. But at this important stage in the evolution of the money system, we must remind ourselves of an important point: *it is the gold that is the money; the paper receipts are not money.*

Gold is money because it is a commodity with accepted value and is convenient to use in exchange. The use of warehouse receipts won't change that. All you receive from the warehouse is a piece of paper, acknowledging that there is gold which belongs to you at the warehouse.

Paper could *not* be useful as money because the relative ease with which it's produced makes it inexpensive by nature; you'd have to use tons of it to obtain the same result served by a few ounces of gold.

The paper takes on value only as it can be exchanged for gold. If the warehouse were to refuse to make gold available, the receipt would eventually be worthless.

It's similar to storing furniture. You can't sit on a furniture receipt; you can only exchange it for something to sit on.

The paper receipts are not money; they are *money substitutes*. They are receipts that can be readily exchanged for real money.*

It is obvious that no one is going to accept a piece of paper just because you want him to. He must be confident that it will eventually bring him what he wants. So there are three essential characteristics required of a worthwhile money substitute, if it is to retain its value:

1. *The warehouse must have a good reputation.* It isn't enough that the receipt holder trusts the warehouse. It must have general acceptance in the market. Otherwise, the holder of the receipt will be limited to exchanging it for gold; he won't be able to trade the receipt to someone else.

2. *The real money must be readily accessible.* If you couldn't exchange your receipt for gold any time you wanted to, what lasting value would the receipt have? And that means...

* Hereafter, I will use the three terms interchangeably: money substitutes, money receipts, and paper money-each meaning receipts that are used in place of real money.

3. *The real money must be kept out of circulation.* If the warehouseman were to spend your gold or lend it to someone else, how could you expect it to be available when you wanted it?

If you hold a receipt, the gold in the warehouse actually belongs to you, not to the warehouse. It would be as preposterous for the warehouseman to use *your* gold as it would be for the Ajax Van & Storage Company to use your furniture while you had it stored there (unless it had your permission).

Imagine, for example, that you walked into a friend's house and found him lying on your sofa. When you expressed your shock, he told you that Ajax had rented your sofa to him because it figured you wouldn't be coming back to get it for a year or so.

Pieces of paper, as titles to commodities, aren't worth much unless you can exchange them at any time of your choosing for the commodity itself.

So to whatever extent any of the three requirements listed above is missing, the money substitute is bound to lose value.

You are paying the warehouseman a fee for a service-the storing of your money. And the gold must be there and accessible for the receipts to have much value.

Along with the normal paper receipts, it is possible to have *tokens*. A token is a money substitute in metallic form, rather than in paper. The present U.S. copper-nickel tokens are a good example.

These are not coins, since there is no significant inherent value (perhaps two cents worth of metal in a quarter). They are money substitutes. Like paper money, they can only have lasting, constant value if they can be readily exchanged for something of real value.

THE DEVELOPMENT OF CREDIT

If the warehouse shouldn't be lending out money that belongs to its customers, how can credit ever develop?

Easily. Suppose you own some gold that you don't intend to spend for awhile. You agree to lend it to your next-door neighbor in exchange for an extra payment (interest) when he returns the gold. Naturally, you know you won't be able to use the money while it is on loan to your neighbor.

The essential ingredient of *real* credit is that one person *gives up* the uses of his money while it is on loan to your neighbor. He is paid interest for temporarily getting along without the money.

Warehouses can play an important part in this. The warehouseman can be aware of who needs money and who has it to lend.

For example, you agree to leave a certain sum of gold in the warehouse for a definite period of time-one year, let us say. To compensate you, the warehouse will pay you interest of 3% on your money.

Now that the warehouseman knows you won't demand your money for a year, he can lend it to another customer at 6% interest-repayable within one year. You have agreed to *give up* the use of the money while the other person has it. You both can't have it to spend at the same time.

In this case, you will not receive a receipt for your gold: because you will have no claim on it for a year. Instead, you will receive a *note* that entitles you to pick up your gold plus interest at the end of the year.

Here we have the difference between *demand deposits* and *time deposits*. A demand deposit is the storing of your money, for which you *pay* a fee-in exchange for the convenience of using receipts. You can demand your money at any time.

A time deposit is the *giving up* of your money for a specified length of time, for which you *receive* a fee-interest.

And, of course, the warehouse is merely the forerunner of the modern-day bank. The bank is a place where people store their money and where savings are lent out to obtain interest. So let's substitute the word *bank* for warehouse; although it won't change any of the principles involved.

No matter what we call the warehouses, you'll produce or exchange only when you believe it will lead ultimately to something you want. You aren't going to give up your production or your property in exchange for a piece of paper you think might be worthless. (It is possible, of course, to trade for a piece of paper that is becoming worthless without you knowing about it.)

If, by now, you've thought to yourself: "My heavens, this is all so painfully obvious," then it will be easier to see how distorted our present-day monetary structure has become when we examine it later on.

What we're reviewing now is obvious-but only in this simplified form. It's not as easy to see these principles amid the complexities of the modern economy, but they still exist.

THE SIZE OF THE MONEY SUPPLY

A number of fallacies have developed regarding the size of the money supply necessary to serve a community.

As with any other commodity, the overproduction of nails or gold or silver (or whatever is the money commodity) will lessen the value of each unit of that commodity in exchange.

This identifies one element in the setting of prices. Suppose one horse and one cow are approximately equal in general market value. If prices are expressed in terms of gold, then the price of each might be five ounces of gold.

If the money supply were somehow doubled, one horse would still be equal to one cow; but both of them would soon be priced at *ten* ounces of gold. Consumers would have more gold to spend but there would have been no increase in the number of products on which to spend it. They would inevitably bid more in order to obtain what they wanted from the limited supply available. And this would cause prices to rise to a level relative to the new, larger money supply.

From this we can formulate an equation that shows how the *general price level* of the community is determined.

At any moment in history, there will be a fixed number of goods and services in the market available for purchase. At the same time, there will be a certain supply of money in the hands of prospective buyers, usable for purchases.

All the goods and services will compete against each other for the available money. And all the monies will compete for the available goods and services.

The general price level will be determined by dividing the available goods and services into the available money, creating a formula:

Available Money Supply

Available Goods and Services = General Price Level

Or, expressed in a different way,

General Price Level=Money divided by Goods

This is an abstract equation-meaning that its only purpose is to help us visualize what's happening. We could never hope to know the exact amount of money available for purchasing at any given moment; nor is there even any way to measure all the horses and cows and TV repair services in any uniform way.

But the equation serves to show us that *the greater the money supply, the higher the prices will be.* Not because a larger money supply makes the products more valuable; but rather because the larger money supply makes the money less valuable. The prices of products are expressed in terms of money. The more money there is, the more will be bid on each item until the supply of available money is used up on the supply of available objects.

This isn't just probable; it's inevitable. If consumers suddenly received gold nuggets that had rained down from heaven, they wouldn't leave prices where they'd been previously. Each consumer would attempt to take advantage of his new apparent wealth to bid more for what he wanted, hoping to bid it away from others.

In the process, prices would invariably go up; the money supply would have increased, but not the available goods and services. No new wealth would have been created (except to whatever extent gold is in demand as a commercial or industrial commodity).

If the money supply decreased, prices would drop. There would not be enough money to buy up the available goods at the old general price level.

Within the general price level, there will be wide variations of prices among the commodities as consumers express their preferences. Some prices will even be dropping while others are going up, as consumers change their minds and rearrange the values they have placed on various items.

But the general price index will necessarily result from the amount of money available for spending and the number of objects available for purchase.

WHAT IS INFLATION?

America is the land of opportunity. So I'm going to suggest that you and I go into business together (at least in your imagination, so I can pose my puzzle to you).

You and I form a partnership, a company that prints counterfeit money. We print 1,000 new $20 bills.

Then we go into San Diego where our affluence (or lack of it) is not known to anyone.

We start spending the bills and are immediately praised by the local merchants and the newspapers.

They proclaim that it is a great thing for san Diego that we have come to town, for we're bringing prosperity to a city that perhaps was in a recession.

Two weeks later, we leave town with $20,000 worth of goods. The townspeople bid us a grateful farewell for all the business we have brought to them.

It's obvious that *we* have benefited from the situation. We traded paper dollars with *no* real value for products that *have* real value.

Assuming that no one ever leans our little secret, has our gain actually hurt anyone else?

In other words, *does anyone every pay for the benefits gained by counterfeiters?*

Set the book down for as long as it takes to think about that question. Did anyone lose in order for us to gain from our counterfeit spree? And, if so, who?

*   *   *

What's your answer?

The merchants who received the counterfeit bills didn't lose. They could pass the bills on to others for things they wanted. (Part of our assumption was that no one would discover the counterfeiting.)

We gained; the merchants didn't lose. Apparently, no one lost.

But we've overlooked a few people. Not just a few, in face. *We've overlooked everyone else in the marketplace.* For everyone else will lose in order to make this gain possible.

We can see this easily as we imagine our car leaving San Diego-loaded with goods removed from San Diego's marketplace. We leave San Diego's residents with less property than they had before we came. There will be fewer goods available to divide up among the people there.

In exchange, they received additional paper money that will circulate in the community. But paper money isn't wealth. It simply means is now *more* paper money to bid for *fewer* goods and services.

Referring back to our price level formula, we see that the general price level is determined by dividing the available goods and services into the available money supply. Since the money supply has gone up and the goods and services have decreased, the result can only be *a higher price level in Sand Diego.*

The price increase will be irregular. Those who get their hands on the counterfeit money first will gain from it; for they'll have extra spending money, and prices won't have gone up yet. But as the extra paper money passes through the community, it will bid prices upward.

The other people in the marketplace will be paying for our gain-*and they will do that through the higher prices they pay for each product.*

Let's carry this example a little further. Suppose our arrival and departure weren't noticed. In other words, no one was aware that an extra $20,000 was suddenly coming into circulation.

The individual merchants who received our $20 bills would have no reason to suppose there was anything unusual or temporary about the increase in business. They'd simply suppose that their long-standing promotional efforts were finally paying off-that success was on its way at last.

They would most likely hire extra clerks to handle the increased business, maybe order a new sign and a better paint job for the store.

And they'd enlarge their inventories to meet the increased demand, of which we appeared to be an example.

But as soon as it became evident that the sudden dose of new business was purely temporary, they'd have to retract their expansion plans. They would lay off the extra clerks and cancel the orders for remodeling.

The painter who was to have done the remodeling would, in turn, have to fire his new helpers. And what would he do with all the extra paint he's ordered?

The net result throughout the area would be a state of gloom. Everyone would have extra commitments to pay off and shelves of undesired stock-all because an illusory boom caused businessmen to gear up to a demand that never really existed.

Would you call that a recession?

Had the businessman understood the artificial nature of their sudden new business, they wouldn't have made their mistaken investments. Instead they'd have recognized the situation for what it was-a sudden, temporary windfall. It was the inability to calculate the true nature of the situation that led to what we think of as a recession.

But let's not get ahead of ourselves. Instead, let me give you another puzzle to ponder, before we go on.

Suppose I've earned 100 ounces of gold by working in the marketplace. Now that I have it, I decide *not* to spend it. I won't even lend it to someone else or put it in the bank. Instead, I go home and bury the 100 ounces of gold in the backyard.

I steadfastly refuse to spend it. Some of my friends (who are Harvard economists) come to me and plead with me to spend the money. "After all," they say, "if you spend it, it'll provide employment for others."

But I still refuse to spend the money. It remains in a hole in the backyard.

What happens as a result? Is anyone *hurt* by my action? If so, who? Does anyone *gain* from my action? If so, who?

Again, set down the book for as long as it takes to ponder the question.

*　　　　　*　　　　　*

What's your answer?

The only possible loser in such a case would be I- the one who has the money and refuses to spend it. Even then, if I have decided (for whatever reason) that I don't want to spend it, you could hardly say that I'm hurt.

But the fact is that I'm simply depriving myself. I've produced something in the marketplace that other people now enjoy. The gold I received was my claim to the goods and services in the market. When I spend the gold, I'm claiming my reward for the things I've already given to others.

If I refuse to exercise that claim, I am the loser-for I'll have fewer goods and services to enjoy. And, in the process, I'll have left that many more goods and services in the market *for others to have.*

This highlights a very popular economic fallacy. Most people believe the market benefits from my *purchase.* But that isn't the case. The market as a whole benefits from my *production,* not my purchase.

When I produce, I add to the total number of goods and services available. When I purchase, I reduce that supply. My purchase is simply a claiming of my reward. If I don't claim it, only I suffer the consequences.

Well then, if I choose to forfeit my reward, who will gain?

Everyone else will profit from me refusal to spend my money. There will be just that many more goods and services left for the others to split up-since I didn't take my share.

And how will that be reflected in practice?

Prices will be affected by the change in the money supply. As I remove 100 ounces of gold from the circulation, prices will drop accordingly (see our price formula). So now everyone can buy *more* goods with the money he already has.

The larger the money supply, the higher the prices are. The smaller the money supply, the lower prices are.

ORGANIZED COUNTERFEITING

In a free market, the gold stock would undoubtedly respond easily and quietly to changes in the volume of goods produced. If the available supply of products increased, prices would drop. That would make each

39

ounce of gold more valuable than it was before, and this in turn would encourage greater production of gold.

On the other hand, if gold were overproduced temporarily, prices would rise and each ounce of gold would be less valuable in exchange. The gold miner would be getting less in return for his efforts. This would discourage production.

Remember: it's *not* the volume of production or the volume of sales that's important to you; it's what you eventually receive for what you've done that counts.

So if gold mining responds smoothly to changes in market needs, the market would seldom ever be disrupted by sudden changes in price levels.

However, an intricate economy (like the one in which we live) will use money substitutes to a much greater degree than real money. And there's plenty of room for manipulation of the money substitutes. It's possible for new paper money to come into circulation without increasing the production or storage of real money.

And this brings us to the next important element in understanding the money system: *inflation.*

Inflation is an increase in money substitutes above the stock of the real money in storage.*

Inflation simply means there are more paper money receipts in circulation than there is real money with

---

* The definitions used in this book have been created by the author. The purpose of a definition is to establish precise communication between author and reader, not to adhere to any authoritative concept. The worth of the definition comes from its ability to draw a sharp line between what *is* certain thing and what isn't. There are several definitions of the word "inflation" in popular use; but this one isolates the one factor that has the greatest effect upon general economic conditions.

which to back them up. As we've seen, this will cause prices to go up. But rising prices are not inflation; they are an *effect* of inflation. Rising prices can result from several different causes (decreased production, for example); but only when they result from an overproduction of paper money do they cause seemingly mysterious changes in the economy.

It is possible for prices to remain stable or even drop during and inflationary period. This would happen if the production of goods increased faster than the increase in paper money (Prices=Money divided by Goods). *But prices would still be higher than they would have been without the inflation.*

We should note also that the price formula will work in the same way whether the *money supply* element refers to real money (gold or silver) or to money substitutes. An increase in money substitutes will cause prices to go up, even if the stock of real money has remained constant; for the formula is affected by whatever is bid for the available goods and services in the market.

Let's return now to the development of our money system. Suppose you left your gold on demand deposit at the bank (warehouse) and received a receipt that you intended to spend in the marketplace. But the banker didn't store the gold; he lent it to someone else-in order to earn interest on money that isn't his. Or perhaps he just issued a second receipt to someone else.

In either case, two people would be trying to spend the gold at the same time. You would have *inflation*-two receipts for the same supply of gold.

One consequence of this would be the well-known "run on the bank." As soon as anyone became suspicious that the banker was doing this, he'd get jittery about his own money.

"Heavens," he'd say, "if there isn't enough gold in the bank to cover every receipt, then someone will be out of luck if everyone decides to turn his receipts for gold. That may not happen-but why take the chance? So, even though I'm a public-spirited citizen who doesn't want to undermine the confidence in our institutions, I have too many humanitarian projects in mind for my gold. So I'd better run down to the bank and get my gold out while there's still some to get!"

If very many people become suspicious, you'd have a run on the bank. And those who arrived there last would be out of luck-if the bank really were cheating on the receipts. If it weren't, everyone would get his gold and the bank's honesty would be proven. This would probably result in increased business for the bank. An honest bank would not have to fear a run.

But if the banker *is* inflating, and can keep that fact hidden, what then? Obviously, he'll draw extra benefits from his ability to lend out gold that doesn't belong to him.

Who will pay for his benefits? The people in the community will pay the difference in higher prices, resulting from the increase of money substitutes in circulation.

The example is no different from our glorious success in San Diego. The paper money supply has been artificially increased and the people in the marketplace will pay higher prices as a result.

The banker has caused inflation in the same way our counterfeiting hit San Diego.

So let's coin another definition of inflation, one more to the point: *Inflation is the counterfeiting of paper money.*

Inflation is the printing of paper money substitutes that aren't backed by real money. And it doesn't matter *who* does the counterfeiting. *Any* increase in paper money-not backed by real money in storage-is going to cause the same reaction: prices will be higher than they would have been without inflation.

Well, we've already come a long way in the development of our money system. We've seen banks or warehouses storing silver and gold, and issuing receipts for them. (They can even store money substitutes and issue checking accounts as a secondary money substitute.)

We've seen coins minted and circulated. Coins are a form of real money; while tokens are money substitutes.

Lending and borrowing take place as one individual gives up the use of his money for a period of time. This can be done through time deposits in banks.

Any bank that issued more receipts than its stock of real money justified would be constantly vulnerable to a "run" that could put it out of business.

Once these runs became common, individuals would probably become disenchanted with *all* banks; for how would you know which ones were honest and which weren't? That would put the burden of proof on the honest banks to *prove* their honesty to the satisfaction of their customers. There are many ways by which that could be done, but it isn't necessary to go into them here.

If the banks overprint the receipts and no bank runs take place (so that inflation continues unchecked), then, as we've seen, prices go up artificially and cause reactions in the marketplace.

We now have all our important elements of a money system at our disposal. So we can leave our island and our warehouses and proceed to modern-day conditions to see what is happening around us.

Our examination of the primitive beginnings of money has been useful to us, however. For it has isolated and identified the principles that exist in any economy. By concentrating on a few elements, we have been able to see them more clearly.

No matter how intricate the economy, no matter how sophisticated "modern economics" may become, some things do not change. For example, *you only produce or exchange when you believe it will lead ultimately to something you want.*

Because of that, actions in the marketplace have reactions, cause have effects, acts produce consequences.

ADVISORY 3

Standard Inflation Hedges

We're ready now to turn our attention to specific investments. In this and the next two chapters, we'll look closely at each of the major types of investments: stocks, bonds, real estate, etc. It's doubtful that any type of investment has been overlooked. Investments made directly in business were covered in the last chapter.

Since there are a large number of investments to be had at (18 types), they've been loosely organized into three major categories: (1) those that are normally considered to be hedges against inflation; (2) those that are normally considered to be hedges against recession or depression; and (3) a group of "independents" that revolve more around gold and silver. One chapter is devoted to each one of these categories.

Each investment will be checked against each of the five basic possibilities we've been following: continued inflation, recession, depression, runaway inflation, and devaluation.

Where an investment group looks good, you'll still have to exercise selectivity within that group, to decide specifically where to place your funds. No attempt is made in this book to recommend specific stocks, etc.

Obviously, your greatest interest will be in looking at those investments you have already or are contemplating at this time. But if you take the time to read all of the three chapters, it should help to reinforce what we've already seen-especially since this will be the practical application of the theoretical ground we've covered.

But, to me, that would be the most foolish course of action. In general, I consider this to be a very bad time to launch any new business that requires a large financial investment.

STOCKS AND MUTUAL FUNDS

Mutual funds are dependent upon stock market movements, so they're included here. We're interested in seeing how stocks in general would perform during any of the possible conditions.*

The stock market is a prime beneficiary of inflation. Miscalculating their resources, many people believe they have extra funds with which to invest, when they really do not. This initiates an upward push in stock prices, attracting other funds from fixed-return investments that don't keep up with inflationary cost-of-living increases.

Continued inflation: Even during good times, I don't consider the stock market to be the welcome haven for the so-called little investor that it's been touted to be. It's a trading ground for professionals who make their living largely off of the small investors who enter the market

*Gold and silver stocks will be considered separately in a later chapter.

Unknowingly. Generally, the small investor (despite professional advice) will buy at the top and sell at the bottom-no matter how hard he tries to do otherwise.

The stock market drop of 1970 should have convinced many people that they didn't belong in the market; but I can only presume that most of them are back again with fresh hopes.

As long as inflation continues at a 6% to 10% annual rate, stock prices will probably stay ahead of that. But it should be recognized that, historically, stock prices have fallen behind when inflation has begun to move faster.

Recession: In any kind of deflation, stock prices drop faster than the general price level drops (the reverse of inflation). The readjustment atmosphere hits the stock market first, even if there's no drop in the general price level. Each recession will be brief, however. It will either respond quickly to reinflation or it will be transformed into a depression.

Depression: When the general price level starts moving downward in earnest, stocks will really tumble. And if you have to sell at the bottom, the price won't be a reflection of the new, lower general price level. Your sale proceeds won't have as much purchasing power as you gave up to buy the stock in the first place.

You'll hear the old cliché that many mutual fund companies and "blue chip" stocks survived the depression and paid dividends right through it. But that's of little comfort. Your resources will be tied up for years waiting for those companies to regain their former prices.

Instead, why not keep your capital liquid and buy at the bottom?

Runaway Inflation: Even though the stock market is a nice hedge against normal inflation, the picture changes drastically when runaway inflation hits. When the currency breaks down, it will put companies out of operation. Who can trade or pay employees without a currency? And there are the possibilities of riots and looting.

Your stock certificates would be worthless under those circumstances. If the company did somehow live through the crisis, there's no guarantee that your property right would be respected in the new order of things. And how would the stock exchange operate without a currency?

Devaluation: Because it's an inflation-oriented investment, the stock market will suffer in the stimulated deflationary conditions following a devaluation. There may be some individual stocks that will gain because the prices of the foreign competitors will have become prohibitive. But the market as a whole would drop much more than most people expect.

There may, however, be a brief period, immediately following the devaluation, when prices will be bid upward. This will be the result of the prevailing ignorance about such things. The market should ultimately drop quite far.

Comments: If you want to be in the stock market, selectivity is important. Prices don't move *en masse*; they fluctuate individually.

But the stock market is no longer a very attractive place for a cautious investor. It's only profitable as long as the present cycle holds; and already we've seen the difficulties encountered in sustaining it during 1969 and 1970.

Since the blow can come at any time, you'll have to have nerves of steel to stay in the stock market now. With what's coming at us like a tidal wave, don't you find it difficult to visualize yourself standing on the beach, waiting for the very last moments before running?

Under the circumstances, *the "blue chip" stock market is for gamblers only today.*

COMMODITIES

This group concerns farm commodities, metals, etc. traded mostly in the futures' markets in Chicago, Los Angeles, and New York.*

The only favorable climate for commodity investment is the present inflationary cycle; and, even there, it is terribly risky. The commodity markets are no place for the part-time investor.

In an interview published in the Los Angeles *Times*, Robert J. O'Brien, chairman of the Chicago Mercantile Exchange, referred to a Department of Agriculture survey indicating that only 25% of all grain speculators made a profit in 1967. He also said that only 2% of all commodity contracts actually reached delivery date. That means 98% of the action comes from speculators; only 2% from actual users or producers of the commodity.* In short, it's a market for professional speculators.

*Silver bullion will be treated separately in a later chapter.

*Los Angeles Times, November 13, 1968.

49

Continued Inflation: If you happen to be a full-time professional, then the market should remain generally bullish as long as the present cycle lasts. Naturally, selectivity is highly important here; specific market conditions of commodities prevent the overall market from moving in any kind of unified fashion.

Recession or Depression: In either case, commodities will suffer. Since so much of the action is speculative, a great deal of paper money will be drained out of the commodity markets during a deflationary period.

Runaway Inflation: The same problem exists here as with the stock market. The commodities markets most likely would close because of an inability to exchange without currency.

Devaluation: Only metals that are traded largely in international markets are likely to profit from a devaluation. Other commodities will probably suffer in much the same way that stocks will. Even if you use silver futures, or some other metal as a hedge against devaluation, your timing has to be very good, if you use margin. On an all-cash basis, or the equivalent, you wouldn't have that to worry about; but there are better ways to hedge against a devaluation.

Comments: There's really nothing to commend the commodities market to the part-time investor. Even if there were, it would be highly vulnerable to governmental intervention. The silver market in New York was closed from 1934 to 1963 as a result of governmental taxing interference. The same thing could happen again.

INCOME REAL ESTATE

This group includes any kind of real estate aimed at drawing income; apartments, rental houses, commercial office buildings, industrial property.

During any inflationary boom, income property always looks attractive. But *overbuilding* is typical in an inflation; and the consequences are rough when the boom is over. There are individual exceptions to this, of course; a medical building isn't quite as vulnerable as a popular-priced resort. But there are other things less vulnerable than medical buildings, too.

Better and better office buildings, more luxurious apartments, frills of all kinds. These are common in an inflation. But they're often unrealistic.

Continued Inflation: If you own income property now, this would be a good time to get rid of it. That doesn't mean the price might not be a little higher next year. But the price might be a great deal *lower* next year; and that's a worse risk.

Current conditions may be all right in general for income property, but it's going to get harder and harder to make rational decisions. Prices and demand signals will begin to get more confusing.

Recession: The extent of the damage done to you during a recession will depend largely upon what kind of tenants you have. If you have tenants who aren't going to be driven out of business by a brief interruption of the inflation, you may whether it all right.

Depression: But here you'll have problems that are much worse. The lowering of the general price level will necessitate lower rents in order to keep tenants. And what if you have a high mortgage on the property? The financial leverage you thought was so attractive can destroy you in a deflation.

This is when the overbuilding shows up. Undoubtedly, there'll be many empty buildings. You'll have no liquidity unless you're willing to sell at a much lower price that at which you bought. And that may not be easy if you have a mortgage.

If creditors are legally allowed to repossess mortgaged property during the depression, that may be an excellent time to purchase property. Homes in relatively well-protected areas would be recommended, since business conditions would remain very uncertain.

Runaway Inflation: This will be totally untenable situation. There'll be no liquidity to your investment. You'll be liable to riots and looting. Tenants will have no currency with which to pay their rents. If you feel you have to stay where you are, be sure you obtain tenants who've saved plenty of silver coins.

Devaluation: With the deflationary conditions involved, money will be drawn away from frills. The time lag between devaluation and sufficient inflation may be too long for you to whether. It will depend mainly upon the kind of tenants you have, as is the case with recession (covered above).

Comments: The only value here is in continued inflation. But even there, it requires perceptive market decisions during a state of confusion. So if it can only be "possibly good" during only the short term, then why get involved?

RESIDENTIAL REAL ESTATE

This section refers only to ownership of your own home. Additional property that's rented to others is covered under *Income Real Estate,* above.

There are two possible reasons why someone would purchase a home. The first is because he desires the control of his own property that home ownership provides. We can refer to this as the *enjoyment value.*

The second reason is because he believes it to be a *profitable investment.* While that *can* be true in some instances, most of the superficial financial benefits turn out to be illusory on closer examination.

You buy a home for $25,000 and sell it a few years later at $35,000, and there seems to be a $10,000 profit. But inflation has caused other prices to go up, and a good part of your apparent profit is just the general price level increase.

In addition, it's easy to overlook the sums of money you've paid out-taxes, repairs, interest, capital improvements, and the like-costs a renter doesn't have to pay. And what about all the wages you should have paid yourself for the labor expended on upkeep?

When all these things are taken into consideration, it's quite likely that your return after selling your home (less broker's commission) will be less in real dollars than what you paid for it. On the other hand, you'll have saved a good deal of rent.

When you put the two together, any profit you have left is *entrepreneurial profit.* That's what you receive for having picked the right house in the right area-in other words, a correct marketing decision. This is the same profit the landlord makes-but only when he happens to be right.

Recognize, too, that if land values in an area are expected to go up (because of some local condition), the price you're expected to pay for the property will already include a good portion of that anticipated higher value.

These remarks aren't made to discourage home ownership, but only to discourage the idea that home ownership is a consistently good financial investment. In the cases where it turns out to be all of that, it's only because of a good marketing decision-the kind you would have to make in any other type of investment in order to profit.

If you're going to buy a home, do it realistically; recognize that you're doing it for the *enjoyment value* that comes from controlling your own property.

Continued Inflation: It doesn't appear that the residential real estate market is a special beneficiary of inflation although inflation-inspired conditions in a given area can cause an increased demand for housing.

If you don't fell the area in which you now live will be comfortable during an economic crisis, now should be the time to sell. It may be that there won't be another period in which it'll be fairly easy to sell.

Recession or Depression: Since the premise here is that home ownership shouldn't be approached as a financial investment, the only relevant consideration is how immobile it makes you. It will be very difficult to liquidate your home during a depression. You may then have a mortgage much bigger than the market value of your home.

If you're intending to keep your present house for the next ten years, and you have a small mortgage or none at all on it, and you're out of the metropolitan areas, then a depression probably won't affect you badly.

But don't overlook the alternative of renting instead and having a pile of cash with which to approach the depression.

As mentioned earlier, it's possible that the government will intervene to bestow "relief" on mortgage payers, at the expense of their creditors. But I wouldn't want to be in the position of counting on either side of that possibility.

Runaway Inflation: If your home is in a metropolitan area, you can only describe the specter of runaway inflation as highly dangerous. You won't be able to sell your home for anything worthwhile; possibly, you'll wind up trading for something that normally has little value.

You'll be vulnerable to chaos and looting. Under those conditions home ownership won't necessarily be synonymous with "having a roof over your head." We've already seen a great deal of painful and costly rioting in America during the past few years. It shouldn't be too hard to visualize the consequences of runaway inflation.

Devaluation: There'll be the same general conditions following a devaluation that accompany a recession. Liquidity will be impaired, but real estate values shouldn't be reduced for too long.

Comments: Here's a suggestion, sort of a double hedge. Sell your home and find a home of comparable quality to rent. Obtain as short a lease as possible. If you had no mortgage on your home, you probably won't like the idea of having to make monthly payments; so deduct five year's rent from the proceeds of the sale and put it in a savings account of the kind that will be recommended in in a later chapter. If you had a mortgage, there's no special reason for you to have your rent payments set aside in advance.

Use the rest of the capital from the proceeds to invest in some of the more conservative aspects of the investment program to be recommended in a later chapter.

If after five years none of what's been projected in this book has come to pass, withdraw your capital from the investment program and buy a home again. Most likely your capital will have appreciated more in the investment program than it would have in your home, possibly enough more to cover the rent payments.

But, most important, this plan will give you flexibility, opportunity, and peace of mind during a time of great uncertainty. With a large investment tied up in your home, you may have trouble sleeping at night. But with your capital totally liquid, you'll be ready to take advantage of any situation that may develop.

When you recognize that home ownership is primarily an enjoyment value, not an investment, you'll probably find that you can rent just about any kind of home you might want.

But if you're determined to own your own home, consider finding an area less vulnerable to some of the chaos that may be ahead.

LAND

"Land booms" are almost always inflation-inspired. The only exceptions are land sales resulting from the discovery of oil or some other permanently valuable resource-a sudden reason, unexpected but realistic, for developing a new area.

This isn't to say that raw land isn't a realistic investment. It can be. But a great deal of the subdividing being done today would have no market without inflation.

In Southern California, for example, residents are bombarded with offers from literally scores of different developers-mostly of desert property. Some of that property may demonstrate a durable value; but most of it is appreciating purely from an inflationary demand.

Land, for most people, could be called an investment frill. It appeals quire largely to income groups that don't do a great deal of investing. But with proper financing and occasional inflationary rises, it has a great attraction as a way of becoming an investor.

In general, land that's been purchased as part of a large subdivision is the most likely to be inflation-inspired investment. So it's most vulnerable to economic crisis.

Continued Inflation: The primary benefit of the *status quo* would appear to be the time it provides for liquidating land investments. Already, individuals are finding it difficult to sell parcels of land purchased in many of the Southern California desert developments.

But whatever the proceeds, they most likely will be more valuable if used elsewhere.

Recession or Depression: Even land in metropolitan areas will have little liquidity during a deflationary period. There's usually very little building during such periods, so land isn't in very much demand. However, if the area looks safe enough to you, it may be profitable to build on your land during a time of extremely low construction prices (if unions and government allow building costs to drop during the deflation).

Runaway Inflation: At least if it's raw land, there's nothing to loot. But you'd have to hold it for the long, long term in order to get anything worthwhile for it. And, in the meantime, you might have trouble protecting your ownership of it.

If the land is in the right place, it might be suitable for a retreat. Put an A-frame on it, stock it with the bare necessities, and have your own resort for vacations-or a retreat, if chaos comes. But don't approach this as a *capital gain.*

Devaluation: There'll be many people trying to sell their land parcels during a post-devaluation period. If you're prepared to wait out that period, the devaluation probably won't affect you one way or the other.

DIAMONDS, JEWERLY, AND ART OBJECTS

For people who like something a little more exotic than the stock market, a good hedge against inflation has always been found among diamonds, jewelry, art objects, antiques, and rare coins.

Continued Inflation: these objects are prime beneficiaries of the inflationary cycle, for the same reason given for other investment frills. But they're primarily the province of professionals who know what they're buying.

Recession: prices will suffer during a recession, even though the general price level may not dip. But it should be a fairly short-term period.

Depression: What was a benefit during inflation will be a bad liability during a depression. Prices will nosedive. Even at low market prices, you may have trouble finding a buyer. These investments can be valuable only if you're prepared to hang on for a long, long time. But why not have your assets in something else of value during the interim, then buy back the art objects later, when they can be purchased for a fraction of their former costs?

Runaway Inflation: Although these were ideal inflation hedges, they're useless for a runaway inflation. You can't liquidate them, with no currency available. You could barter them only for very large purchases, if you could even find a prospect. Otherwise, you couldn't spend them. How do you make change for a 3-carat diamond?

Devaluation: Diamonds that are sold freely in international markets can be a source of profit from a devaluation. They'll appreciate in dollars from the change in currency rates. Manufactured jewelry and art objects may not be as valuable, unless they can be sold easily in foreign markets soon after devaluation.

Comment: Despite the glamorous nature of these investments, they're mostly inflation hedges. And its time to start switching to depression hedges and runaway inflation hedges.

STANDARD DEPRESSION HEDGES

During an inflationary period, depression hedges never appear very attractive. But Andrew Carnegie claimed that one of the cornerstones of his success was his ability to develop a strong cash position during inflationary times. He then used it to buy up facilities and goods during deflationary periods.

That philosophy is still sound today. However, the government is making each succeeding depression a little stickier than the previous one; and there are pitfalls to be avoided, which we'll recognize as we proceed.

CASH AND SAVINGS ACCOUNTS

Carnegie probably didn't show much return on his cash position while he was accumulating it during inflationary periods. But his incentive wasn't the interest rate. His purpose was to acquire liquidity for the times he knew were coming.

Continued Inflation: The latest credit squeeze in 1969 is evidence that savings accounts can't keep up with inflation. The only justification for a savings account is its liquidity. But that can be more than enough-provided you're sure the cash will be available in all circumstances.

Recession: Cash isn't as good as might be expected. As mentioned before, there probably will be very little drop in the general price level, if any. There will be liquidations, but possibly not of the things you'd want to buy.

Depression: But here cash comes in its own. Then the lower price level would make it possible to acquire some potentially good investment. However, the normal value of cash the consumer goods might be neutralized by minimum price levels enforced by the government. It's less likely that capital goods and investments would be price-supported.

Runaway inflation: As others have said, if runaway inflation comes, I hope your home is decorated in green; because your cash will be useful only as wallpaper. Once you see prices moving every day or two, get rid of whatever cash you have as fast as possible.

Devaluation: Despite the simulated deflation, prices won't drop much; so your cash won't be of any special value. There'll be some business liquidations; but probably not anything you would want to acquire.

Once there's a devaluation, you should especially alert to the possibility of runaway inflation following.

Comment: Since bank holidays can never be legislated out of existence, be careful about normal savings accounts. Despite the loss of interest, keeping cash somewhere safe (other than in a U.S. bank) will allow you to sleep more easily.

BONDS AND TREASURY BILLS

Included in this group are bonds of governmental agencies, corporate bonds, and U.S. Treasury bills.

Continued Inflation: The interest paid on the bonds is comparable to what your losing through inflation. So you're just breaking even.

Recession: The value of the bond would remain somewhat stable, and you'd continue to draw the interest.

Depression: this is the one eventuality for which bonds are attractive. The redemption value would remain stable while the general price level is falling. As a result, this is a traditional hedge against depression.

But there's always the threat that if times get hard enough (and they might), the government can default on its promise to pay off the bonds.

Wouldn't they do that? It's been done before (always with proper "justification," of course).

Runaway Inflation: Treasury bills and bonds are liquid in any other situation; but in runaway inflation, they'll be totally worthless.

Devaluation: All things considered, bonds wouldn't be affected much.

Comment: Bonds are only of advantage if you're sure we're headed straight for a depression. Even then your timing must be pretty good; for bonds fluctuate in price after they're issued. If you can buy them when they're underpriced, they can be better than cash. Convertible bonds have additional alternatives, but these alternatives don't cover all the possibilities we're concerned with here.

MORTGAGES AND OTHER LOANS

Traditionally, it's better to be a debtor during inflation and a creditor during deflation. There are pictures of the "penny-pinching" bankers who get rich in a depression by foreclosing mortgages. Factually, the picture leaves a lot to be desired, however.

The banker doesn't show much profit during a depression. He hasn't been lending his own money. Rather, he's been borrowing at one interest rate and lending at a higher interest rate. The difference is in his profit.

When an economic crisis occurs, those who have claims against him exercise those claims. Depositors want their money. But his capital is tied up in long-term loans that can't be called unless the borrower defaults.

If the borrower should default, the home can be repossessed. But the recovered asset is usually worth less than the mortgage at the time. Sure, the banker has acquired some homes-but it'll be years before they'll be worth anything.

This same principle applies, whether it's a bank, savings and loan, mortgage company, or any other form of lending agency.

In addition, governments traditionally intervene on the side of the debtors during hard times. As far back as the depression of 1819, state governments passed various laws to prevent creditors from receiving payments due them.

Continued Inflation: There's and obvious erosion of your investment in an inflationary cycle. When you're repaid, the dollars you receive will buy less than those you originally lent. Purchasing trust deeds at a discount helps to compensate for this, but they aren't bargains. The discount is merely a recognition of the depreciating value and the high risk involved in such a transaction. And the interest runs a race with the rising general price level.

Recession: Probably the only time when an individual can actually repossess property advantageously is during a recession. The short-term readjustment period can cause a borrower to default; and the depressed real estate market will probably rebound with the next bout of inflation. But if your timing is bad, and it's really the advent of a depression, you'll have a white elephant in your hands.

Depression: If you foreclose on a $15,000 mortgage and repossess a house that's worth only $12,00 in the current market, how have you gained? You'd have been much better off to have held on to your original $15,000.

Your only hope is that your borrowers continue to make their payments. If they *do*, what you will receive will have appreciated in value, thanks to deflation. But it's a very risky business.

Runaway Inflation: Obviously, this works to your disadvantage. The borrower can pay you off in cheap dollars any time he chooses.

Devaluation: The simulated deflation will create similar circumstances to that created by a recession.

Comment: There's too much uncertainty connected with any of the possibilities to make this an attractive investment.

LIFE INSURANCE AND RETIREMENT PLANS

This concerns life insurance as an investment. That means whole life policies, annuities, endowments, retirement plans, pension programs, etc.

In cash-value insurance policies, the premium includes two components: what you're paying for the life insurance itself and what you're paying into a savings account that's drawing interest.

This isn't a discussion of the value of life insurance itself; we're viewing only the savings account part. To determine how much is involved, subtract the cost of a comparable term insurance policy from the premium of you cash value policy.

Continued Inflation: As long as the interest earned on your cash value savings can keep up with inflationary increases in the general price level, you're breaking even. But we're probably past that point already, in which case you may actually be losing money.

Recession: Here you have a relatively stable value plus interest.

Depression: The traditional value is the increased buying power of a fixed amount of dollars while prices are falling. Most insurance companies should survive a depression, just as they did before. But there has to be a point at which their investments in inflation-inspired land holdings can destroy them.

Runaway Inflation: Your policy would be worthless; because there'd be no currency with which the insurance company could pay you.

Devaluation: Theoretically, you shouldn't be affected one way or the other. But we've already seen that a devaluation will encourage the trend toward runaway inflation. And since life insurance policies are usually undertaken for the long term, it will require some will power to get out of the policy when it becomes evident that you should.

Comment: The only value is for deflationary possibilities. Even in continued inflation, you're losing.

It'd make more sense to convert to term insurance. Determine the amount of protection you'd want your beneficiary to have; then ass 50% for inflation. There's no reason to add more than %50; for beyond that, the economy will be headed toward making your policy worthless.

Most companies won't allow you to convert your cash value policy to term insurance without taking out a new policy (physical examination, etc.). So it'd be wise to make the change now, rather than wait until some time in the future when you may be less able to qualify. In closing out your cash value policy, you'll be paid the accumulated value of your policy to that date.

SELLING SHORT

"In 1929, I sold short." In the popular song, those words describe the man who does everything right. Anyone who sold short before the crash probably made a fortune. The word "probably" is appropriate, however, because there are factors of stock selection, timing, etc., involved.

Obviously, the time to sell short is just before a deflation. Since news of credit restrictions always brings a speculative sell-off in the market, you lose a good deal by waiting for such obvious indicators. However, if you know what you're going to do in advance, and then execute it immediately upon hearing such news, you'll probably reap most of the benefit.

The individual stocks to select would be those with the most "air" in their prices, usually those with the highest price earnings ratios. In other words, the stocks that have been helped most by inflation will probably drop the fastest in a deflation.

Continued Inflation: Not the time for this, of course.

Recession: Useful perhaps as a period in which to test your ability to pick the right stocks for short selling.

Depression: This is the best time. Somewhere along the way, as the stocks start dropping, an "air pocket" is hit where there are *no* buyers and the price drop is straight down.

Runaway Inflation: No.

Devaluation: This may be a real sleeper. As we've seen, there'll be a simulated deflation after the devaluation (dependent upon the amount of dollars still spent on imports). There are many opinions expressed about the effects of a devaluation, but few people recognize the deflationary possibilities.

Prices in general won't fall; but stock prices, in general, will. With a good selection of stocks, a short seller might do surprising well at this time.

In addition, the readjustment period caused by the devaluation could plunge the economy into a depression. If that happens, the timing will have proven it to be ideal.

If you decide to do this, pick your stocks now. Choose the prime beneficiaries from inflation, those most likely to plummet in the deflationary post-devaluation period.

Once the devaluation happens, watch the stocks continuously from a broker's office. The stocks will probably continue to climb for awhile. But when one drops 5% from its post-devaluation high, sell short (or place a put). That should be your best timing. If it then rises 10%, cover your *short* and take your loss.

Comment: Short selling is a glamorous idea, and there *will* be some fortunes made along the way. But it really isn't appropriate for a part-time investor. It'll require full-time attention, careful selection, good timing, and an iron constitution. It's a go-for-broke idea- recommended for bachelors only.

If you do get involved, consider using puts (options to sell) rather than selling outright. It's a hedge against your own mistakes. It'll reduce your own mistakes. It'll reduce your potential profit, but the insurance is worth it.

"REAL MONEY" HEDGES

The time when you should acquire real money (gold and silver) is when it's generally respected the least. When governments are abandoning gold and silver, when the "experts" are saying that we can get along without them, when people don't seem to care one way or the other-that's the time when you'd better turn your assets into gold and silver.

For that's the time when the most unrealistic monetary ventures will be undertaken. Currencies will fail; savings will be destroyed. The future will be rebuilt by those who were smart enough to ignore the mass psychology.

Real money means gold and silver. But that isn't the end of it. As we saw in the second chapter, the man who produces the money commodity has no inside track to wealth. There are inefficient gold miners, just as there are inefficient druggists.

In this chapter we'll examine three investments based upon gold, three based upon silver, and one that's somewhat related. Some of these investments look better than others; and even the favored ones require further selectivity.

SILVER BULLION

Some have asked whether silver coins will disappear. The answer is very definitely-No. Our present coins will won't disappear, and they won't even become rarities . . . if anybody has any idea of hoarding our silver coins, let me say this. Treasury has a lot of silver on hand, and it can be, and it will be used to keep the price of silver in line with its value in our present silver coin. There will be no profit in holding them out of circulation for the value of their silver content.

President Lyndon B. Johnson, July 23, 1965*

The president was saying, in effect, that the price of silver wouldn't go over $1.29 per ounce, the monetary price of silver. His confidence was based upon a hoard of silver that the U.S. Treasury had accumulated over a 90-year period. As long as the U.S. government was willing to sell silver to anyone in the world at $1.29 per troy ounce, there was no way the price could go higher.**

But contrary to many such governmental forecasts, on May 17, 1967, the Treasury announced it no longer had enough silver to continue selling worldwide at $1.29. It limited its sales to privileged American industrial buyers. The price *did* move upward; and the silver coins *did* stay hidden.

In terms of yearly production versus yearly consumption, the world had been short of silver for several years. As long as the Treasury hoard could make up the difference, there was no apparent shortage. But once the government curtailed its sales, the shortage became critical.

For the next year, the price rose fairly steadily, reaching a high of $2.55 in May 1968. Then the Treasury loosened its grip on the remaining reserves and more silver flowed

*. At the signing of the new coinage act-quoted in the Annual Report of the Director of the Mint, 1965.

**. Gold and silver are always weighed in terms of *troy* ounces, rather than avoirdupois ounces. All references to ounces in this book are troy ounces.

Into the market, sending the price downward. By October 1968 it was back in the $1.80 range; and, with slight fluctuations up and don, it remained in that range into 1971.

During 1968, the Treasury accumulated around 200 million ounces of silver coins, which it then melted and sold to industrial silver users. By leveling off the weekly sales at two million ounces, it managed to keep the market in balance.

The Treasury predicted it would continue doing this for several more years (just as it had earlier predicted it could hold the price at $1.29 into the 1970s); but there was nowhere near enough silver in the till to back that up.

In the spring of 1969, the government lifted its ban on the private melting of silver coins, to prepare the way for its own withdrawal from the market.

Finally, on November 10, 1970, it sold silver to the market for the last time. This reduced the availability of silver by 75-100 million ounces per year. After the silver users' reserves have been exhausted, the upward pressure on the price of silver should begin.

Silver is in far shorter supply throughout the world than the government has been willing to admit. Rising prices won't stimulate production-for two reasons: (1) silver isn't widely available to be produced; and (2) 80% of the silver produced comes as a by-product of the production of lead, zinc, copper, or gold. Why would a copper miner, who derives maybe 10% of his revenue from silver, increase his production-just because the price of silver is rising.

On the other side of the market, industrial consumers have found no acceptable replacements for any of the more important uses of silver' and it's very unlikely that they'll do so in the next few years. Consequently, their demand for silver won't be reduced by higher prices.***

It wouldn't be surprising to see the price of silver in the $4.00 to $6.00 range in the early seventies (augmented by whatever inflation does to the general price level).

Continued inflation: As the above information indicates, the price of silver bullion should appreciate over the next two to three years, based purely upon market considerations.

Recession: It will be affected by any brief readjustment period, when speculation inevitably will be pinched-for the same reasons that stocks will.

***. The economics of the silver situation are summarized in Smith: *Silver Profits in the Seventies* and Rickenbacker: *Wooden Nickels.*

Depression: It's very possible that silver prices might benefit from a depression. Industrial use will drop, but probably not as much as production-since the latter is so dependent upon copper, lead, and zinc production, traditional losers in a depression. This could increase the shortage.

At the same time, however, the general price level will be dropping, including that of silver prices. Again, silver and gold are havens in times of uncertainty. So it's difficult to say how all these factors will combine to affect the silver price in a depression. If there's a drop, it shouldn't be very great.

Runaway Inflation: Silver would weather a hyperinflation. It's even liquid during a crisis, if you take your proceeds in a foreign currency that's unaffected.

Devaluation: As we saw earlier, the price of silver will appreciate in dollars in proportion to any unilateral dollar devaluation. Silver is an attractive devaluation hedge.

Since you can buy bullion on margin, you can use a portion of your assets to protect all of them.

Comments: Silver bullion is one of the best all-around investments, especially for what we'll probably be facing in the next few years. You'll be protected against any possible disasters. In fact, you'll *profit*-whatever direction the economy might take, including a continuation of the *status quo.*****

It's well within the realm of possibility that the U.S. government could one day confiscate private holdings of silver, as it did gold. Certainly the government has shown that much interest in silver in the past. If you don't want to take a chance, keep your bullion outside of the United States.

Silver bullion should be bought for present delivery. Stay out of the futures' market, for all the reasons indicated in the section on commodities as mentioned earlier.

With the exception of gold, there's no particular attraction in any other precious metal (platinum, palladium, etc.).

GOLD BULLION

American citizens and other residents of the U.S. are legally prohibited from owning gold bullion, here or anywhere else in the world. Since it's possible that this book may be read by individuals outside the United

---

**** Jerome F. Smith first called my attention to several of the above considerations.

States, we'll examine gold bullion as we have other investments.

Just as the U.S. government kept the price of silver down to $1.29 for many years, so it held down the price of gold. The government made it a policy to sell as much gold in the free market as was necessary to keep the price from rising above $35.00 per ounce (which is, automatically, the official gold price in any other currency also.) Whenever the demand for gold threatened to push the price upward, our government unloaded some of its reserves-to meet the demand and prevent a price increase.

Finally, in 1968, a full-scale run on gold threatened to wipe out the American gold supply. A hasty solution was adopted: governments would settle international trade balances by exchanging gold with each other at the official redemption rates ($35.00 and its equivalent in other currencies); but there'd be no more attempts to hold down the free market price with governmental gold reserves.

The governments of the Western nations pledged not to sell any of their gold reserves in the free market (to take advantage of the higher prices there). Suddenly there was a really free market in gold, since our government was no longer dumping its reserves there to hold down the price. Since then, the price has fluctuated, hitting a high of $42.00 per ounce.

Continued Inflation: Gold is real money; and that's what people turn to, if they can, when inflation runs rampant. Citizens, of France, West Germany, and a few other countries buy gold when their own governments get out of line. In addition, since so much seems to depend upon the United States, continued inflation here adds to the worldwide demand for gold.

The free market price isn't necessarily going to go straight up, however. In late 1969, it dropped back to $35.00 per ounce when chances of an early dollar or pound devaluation temporarily lessened. There'll be many such fluctuations-but the overall trend should move upward.

Recession: The gold market is a worldwide market; so a U.S. recession probably won't affect gold bullion adversely. If anything, it could encourage foreign investors to get into gold, until the uncertainty ends.

Depression: If the depression is worldwide, prices of most everything will fall. Gold prices would be supported somewhat by the flight to gold in crisis times. On balance, gold should profit; but it's not certain.

Runaway Inflation: Gold is an ideal asset during a runaway inflation, provided your gold is stored in a safe place. It's liquid if you take your proceeds in a currency that isn't suffering from the crisis.

Devaluation: A doubling of the redemption rate for dollars will double the price for gold in the free market, so gold bullion is a prime beneficiary of devaluation.

Comments: There's good reason for non-U.S. citizens to include gold bullion in their investment programs. But an American citizen would have to violate the law. The investment program recommended later will cover most everything that owning gold bullion would have done for him, however.

Since gold isn't a scarce commodity, in the way that silver is, it doesn't have the same supply-and-demand pressure to push the price upward. And most of the monetary factors that will send gold upward should eventually affect silver anyways.

GOLD STOCKS

Because gold and silver are particularly important, and because gold and silver stocks are likely to move contrary to the general market, these stocks are treated individually here, instead of being included earlier.

Hear again, as with other investment groups, selectivity is important. In fact, *especially* here-since there's definite value in holding gold stocks. Further investigation will be necessary to find the individual companies whose stocks represent the best buys. The mere fact that a firm mines gold doesn't mean it's efficient, durable, or that its stock is a bargain at present prices.

Once you've found the gold stocks that are priced right and are durable, the following considerations apply:

Continued Inflation: Gold stocks should continue to appreciate in the present economic climate. We now have a free market in gold; the gold prices should seek its own level and then continue to appreciate as currencies depreciate further.

There'll be intense monetary speculation in gold-causing some wide fluctuations, as currencies look dim, then revive.

All of these factors will invariably affect the prices of gold stocks. But the ultimate attraction of gold stocks will be the inevitable devaluation and, possibly, the eventual worldwide adjustment of gold prices.

In the meantime, some South African stocks are paying dividends of 6-10%. So these stocks are usually attractive, even without a devaluation.

Recession: Since there's been a true free market in gold only since 1968, there's been little precedent by which one can predict the reactions of gold stocks to various phenomena. If you own South African gold stocks, and the recession is in the United States, the effect *should* be upward pressure on the prices. This would come as a result of the uncertainty generated by the U.S. recession, with little of the deflationary reflects upon the South African price levels (except as U.S. citizens provide a market for those stocks).

Depression: Here the lack of a precedent creates a mystery. With deflation affecting speculation on the one hand, and the flight to gold from uncertainty on the other, we seem to have a toss-up. However, the precedents that *do* exist demonstrate that gold stocks run counter to prevailing trends. The gold price remains constant while costs drop. The stock of Homestake Mining had a low in inflationary 1928 of $40. It's high during 1937 (the depth of the depression) was $10,80. Much of this increase was due to the devaluation of 1934, however.

Runaway Inflation: Gold stocks will survive hyperinflation, provided the companies involved aren't in the nation suffering the runaway inflation. There may not be absolute liquidity during the crisis. But after the run is over, the demand for gold should be even greater-as a result of the graphic example of the crisis.

If you hold stock in a company in the nation suffering runaway inflation, sell it at the first danger signal.

Devaluation: With a change in U.S. redemption rates to $70 to $105 (or anything else), the free market price of gold does *not* automatically change. Neither does the price of gold change in any other currency. It will be only the *dollar price* that changes.

Consequently, the dollar price of gold bullion will increase and the price paid in dollars to an American gold mining company will go up. *But it won't necessarily affect any companies in nations where devaluation hasn't occurred.*

In South Africa, the gold mining companies sell their output to the government, which, in turn, markets the gold to the world. Those companies can only profit from a devaluation if the south African government changes its *own* redemption rate. And the South African government has very little incentive to do that.

If the U.S. government devalues to a $70 per ounce basis, it will double the number of dollars South Africa will get for each ounce of gold sold to the United States. That means a doubling of the goods it can buy from the United States, without increasing its own output in any way. South Africa's chief export is gold; the small harm done to other South America exports will be incidental, compared to the gain realized on god trading.

It appears to official policy for the South African government to pass on any such benefits to the gold companies. But the only sure way those companies can benefit is by higher free market demand for the bullion itself-not by changes in redemption rates, which do nothing more than change currency ratios.

Because currencies are receipts for gold, visualizing the effects of devaluation on the various prices for gold can be a tricky business. I must admit that, for a long time, I assumed that South African gold companies would automatically profit from a dollar devaluation.

But for the reasons just outlined, the South African *companies* are the poorest bets-if you're counting on a devaluation for their ultimate profits. As a group, their stocks are holding up well in price, in anticipation of a devaluation; but only because most speculators are incapable of visualizing the effects of a devaluation. The stocks most likely will sky-rocket in a mistaken post-devaluation hysteria. But eventually those prices would have to collapse.

In an earlier chapter, we saw the three-step post-devaluation process by which silver (for example) would increase its dollar price, then slip back in all currencies. That's because the higher dollar price reduces buying pressure from the United States.

The same thing will be true of gold. Higher dollar prices for gold will be reflected I the free market-as far as Americans are concerned. This will discourage American demand. Also, there should be especially large sell-off by those who've anticipated the devaluation correctly. These two factors would apply downward pressure on the free market price.

The ultimate result *could* be a dollar price for gold in the market that would be *less* than the U.S. government's new redemption rate (but higher than the previous rate). That would take *all* the pressure off the government's gold supply for awhile. (And it would really encourage further inflation.)

Summarizing the preceding data, it's recommended that an American gold stock be bought to assure full profit from a dollar devaluation. And South African stocks should be bought because their prices will probably go sky-high from purely emotional and unrealistic reactions right after the devaluation.

When that happens, watch all of your stocks continually during trading hours. *Sell a stock automatically when it has dropped 5% from its post-devaluation high.*

In so doing, you *may* miss its final high. But chances are you'll come very close. In addition, the higher post-devaluation profits from American gold mining companies will make them extremely vulnerable to government intervention. That's another reason I'd rather be out as early as possible.

There's another fallacy that should be dealt with. You could call it the "multiple earnings fallacy." It goes like this: Ajax Gold Mining Company (a fictional company) sells gold in the free market at approximately $40 per ounce. At this rice, it makes $3 per ounce net profit and pays a pretty fair dividend. If the price of gold goes to $70 per ounce, it won't change the company's costs at all. So its profit per ounce will jump from $3 to $33, an elevenfold increase. If the price of gold doubles, the stock will more than double; it will go up about 11 times.

The fallacy is in thinking that the company's costs won't go up. As we saw earlier, that isn't the case. Higher prices mean higher costs-not the reverse, as is commonly thought. The company whose profits are going up will begin to bid higher for workers and equipment in the market, hoping to produce more and get a larger share of the higher-priced market.

And in this case, it'll be bidding primarily against its own competitors-*who have the same extra bidding power.* This will neutralize part of the added profits.

This doesn't mean that earnings won't go up. They definitely will. But don't get carried away and expect them to go up in a geometric progression.

Many investors *will* be waiting for those higher dividends, however; and they may temporarily bid the stock unrealistically high.

Comments: Even though an American gold stock is more likely to gain, it is *not* an unmixed blessing. Any gold companies are subject to government pressures, regulation, and even the possibility of nationalization.

In buying gold stocks, recognize the risks you're taking and be moderate in your investment. Buy both American and South American stocks for diversification. Even if one group loses, the gains of the other group should more than offset that.

SILVER STOCKS

In general, silver stocks should parallel changes in the price of silver bullion. Most of what was said regarding silver bullion applies here. But, just as with gold stocks, there'll be differences in performance between various companies.

Continued Inflation: Silver-producing companies should profit from the supply-and-demand factors that were reviewed earlier.

Recession: Silver stocks would probably decline in a brief recession, along with most other stocks.

Depression: As mentioned earlier, the price of silver will probably go up after the depression has been underway for several months. This should increase the value of those companies that produce silver exclusively.

Runaway Inflation: The stock can only be useful if the company survives intact; and it isn't likely to survive a runaway inflation. In addition, the stock exchanges would be closed.

Devaluation: If the dollar price of silver goes up, American companies will profit from the devaluation. But beware of the "multiple earnings" fallacy that was detailed earlier.

Comments: Only an American company would profit from a dollar devaluation. And American companies are too vulnerable to regulation and nationalization.

In addition, the price-earnings ratios are generally very high on those stocks that are already producing silver. Those companies that aren't yet in production will have to wait a very long time before showing profits and dividends.

There's nothing a silver stock can do that silver bullion can't do; and silver bullion lacks some of the vulnerabilities of the stocks. So bullion looks much more attractive.

SILVER COINS

There are two distinct markets for silver coins. Although it isn't generally recognized, they're entirely different markets.

As we've seen, most of the silver coins disappeared from circulation during 1964-1965, because of inflation. Two years later, the price of silver finally sprang loose from $1.29 per ounce. As a result, silver-in all forms-was suddenly in greater demand.

Thus silver coins have a value in two ways: (1) they can be melted down, the silver content refined, and sold on the market as *bullion*; and (2) they are *silver coins* with all the values of a true coin (recognizable weight and fineness). Once melted the silver no longer has its coin value, but takes on value as bullion.*****

In either case, it's the silver content that makes the coin valuable. But this expresses itself in two ways: as a coin (a "real money" medium of exchange) and as *potential bullion*.

Continued Inflation: In the current economy, silver coins' profit from both markets. They'll rise in value on the coat tails of silver bullion; and, as coins, they'll become more valuable as inflation becomes even more pronounced.

Recession: There might be a slight drop in value during a brief recession.

Depression: Silver coins shouldn't be thought of as cash buying power for purchasing at the depths of a depression. Cash is always acquired at face value. The face value will buy more as prices drop.

But you can't acquire silver coins today at face value (except for a stray dime or quarter given you in change here or there); in early 1971, you paid the face value plus about 30%. So the general price level has to drop that 30% first, before any further price drop can increase the buying power of the face value of coins.

However, the bullion potential of the coins may go

*****We are referring here to what is called "junk silver"-silver coins that have no numismatic value. Coins of specific, valuable dates are treated under "Diamonds, Jewelry, and Art Objects."

up, for reasons mentioned before.

Runaway Inflation: For this possibility, silver coins are an absolute necessity. They'll be the only spendable money around. Particularly useful will be the dimes and quarters-as opposed to half-dollars or silver dollars. The lower units give you more liquidity.

Devaluation: The bullion potential will profit, for the reasons we've already reviewed. The coinage value will become more critical, too, because of the likelihood that stepped-up inflation will follow.

Comments: Buy silver coins as the ultimate hedge against runaway inflation. There are dealers who sell the coins in $1,000 bags and finance them. The bags are stored in a bank. That's a different kind of investment, and it may be used in the place of silver bullion. We'll discuss it further in a later chapter. Here we're concerned with silver coins as the ultimate form of spending money.

Keep the coins at home, think of them as a form of absolute security, not as a traditional profit-making investment.

GOLD COINS

It's illegal for American citizens and other residents of the United States to own gold bullion. But it *is legal*, at this time, to own gold coins of any nation, *provided they are dated 1933 or earlier* (because they're considered collectors' items).

This is a way for Americans to own gold. However, you pay a premium price, mainly because the gold is more valuable in the form of coins.

Continued Inflation: With a free market in gold, they should continue a basic long-term trend upward.

Recession: Again, we have the problem of a lack of precedents, because there was no true free market in gold prior to 1968. But you could expect the dollar price to drop somewhat in an American recession.

Depression: As with gold bullion, it's difficult to forecast precisely what gold coins would do in a depression. Most likely, they'll break even or go up in price.

Runaway Inflation: Gold coins would be far less useful than silver coins as spending money, because of their higher value per unit. But once you've stored enough silver coins, you can save gold coins for large purchases of property, capital goods, businesses, or anything else. The holder of a large supply of gold coins may be in the position to create a new fortune after the chaos is over and rebuilding has begun.

Devaluation: the coins are bound to reflect the higher bullion prices. They can be an excellent replacement for the individual who's legally prevented from owning gold bullion.

Comments: American coins are general preferable too foreign coins-because the gold content will be more easily recognizable. However, some foreign coins are priced closer to their gold contents.

SWISS FRANCS AND OTHER
FOREIGN CURRENCIES

This type of investment is included in this chapter because it serves the same basic purpose as gold or silver.

The only currency to be recommended is the Swiss franc. Other countries run hot and cold. The German mark has been popular until recently-but no more so than the French franc had been in 1967. And the French franc certainly has gone sour in the interim.

Strangely, the Swiss franc doesn't have the stable value it's often thought to possess. Heavy shipments of money into Switzerland create inflationary conditions, causing volatile changes in the currency exchange rates. Switzerland is a small country, so foreign investors can cause imbalances in the Swiss economy.

Yet, through it all, the Swiss franc is a safe currency, backed up solidly by gold. Whereas the American dollar is really only 4% backed by gold, the Swiss franc is 83% backed by gold. With that much difference, it's apparent that the statement "If the dollar is devalued, all other currencies will be, too" is very realistic. Why should the Swiss devalue such a sound currency?

There's a vast difference between the currencies.

SWISS FRANC PAPER MONEY SUPPLY

(converted for comparison into dollar equivalents)

(October 1968)

Current Account Deposits:	$ .7 billion
Currency in Circulation:	<u>$2.5 billion</u>
Total Money Substitutes:	$3.2 billion
Monetary Gold Stock:	$2.6 billion

(Source: Swiss National Bank)

The Swiss record of currency management is the best in the world. Historically, Swiss bankers and politicians refuse to play the typical monetary games that are so common to other countries. I find it hard to conceive of the Swiss rushing to the rescue of the American dollar when things get rougher. The Swiss government doesn't even belong to the International Monetary Fund.

Continued Inflation: By keeping the Swiss francs in a Swiss bank. You'll earn between 4% and 5% interest. That's about what you can get in a savings account here, but hardly an attractive rate. But if the American inflation speeds up, a 5% rate on Swiss francs will actually be larger when converted back to dollars. So you don't need to fear any great inflationary loss of value. The main reason for such an account is to maintain liquidity.

Recession: Since we're not expecting much of a change in the purchasing value of the dollar during a short-term recession, you'll neither win nor lose by having the Swiss francs.

Depression: Here you'd lose some purchasing power, since the dollar would probably gain in value. But you'd have greater security and liquidity in the Swiss franc; and that means greater peace of mind-which should make the loss worthwhile. The chances of a Swiss bank failing aren't nearly as great as those of an American bank.

Runaway Inflation: The Swiss franc would certainly preserve your store of value; but during the few days of the actual runaway period, there'd be no liquidity. You wouldn't want to convert and francs back into dollars because they'd immediately lose their value.

But as soon as the run were over and any new medium of exchange developed, the francs would be liquid, whereas many other types of investments we've seen wouldn't be.

This would give you resources with which to acquire articles of wealth, once some stability had been restored to the community.

Devaluation: It is possible (although not probable) that the Swiss franc will be devalued eventually. But it certainly won't be devalued in the absence of a dollar devaluation; nor will it suffer a larger devaluation. If there's a simultaneous readjustment of currency ratios, the Swiss franc will probably have the smallest devaluation.

If the dollar is devalued, and not the Swiss franc, you may want to protect yourself by quickly converting your Swiss francs back into dollars. There's always the chance of a Swiss franc devaluation *following* the dollar devaluation. Since there's little chance of two dollar devaluations in quick succession, you have everything to gain and nothing to lose.

Comment: The principal value of the Swiss franc is in their cash liquidity and their invulnerability to both U.S. banks and U.S. dollar devaluation.

ADVISORIES 4

Inflation Starts To Gallop

So the government's inflation didn't produce prosperity, after all. It simply distorted our choices temporarily.

Why, then, bother to pump inflation into the economy in the first place? Because those who control the inflation (the banks and the government) benefit so much from it. And, usually, those who are first in line at the subsidy window are the most vocal elements in the market.

The government invokes inflation as a way of appearing to create prosperity-as a way of financing, on a subtle basis, its own programs. Once underway, the inflationary program must be sustained in order to ward off the recession that will inevitably follow.

The additional inflation is simply postponing the day of reckoning. And it's covering up a greater and greater number of miscalculations that must come to light eventually. These mistakes can't be hidden forever; but the government hopes they can (or at least until another administration is in office).

And so the binge continues, guaranteeing an even *worse* readjustment period ahead. The longer the cycle lasts, the bigger the inflation, the greater number of miscalculations to be liquidated, the worse the recession to come.

But now another element enters the picture. As the money managers attempt to continue the cycle, they find that their doses of inflation don't have the effect they once had. Certainly our anti-hero Joe Consumer, isn't going to be fooled by another $100 raise; he's wise now.

And, through all this, *the consumer is in a daze.* His concept of his buying power is totally distorted. He sits by his swimming pool, eating a can of beans for dinner. He drives to work in a new car, while his children go without dental care and his furniture falls apart.

Not surprisingly, many individuals begin to think less of themselves, feeling incapable of coping with life in an efficient manner.

The consumer finds himself turning more and more to credit as a means of keeping up with himself. He continually plans ahead, seeing the day when he'll be out of debt. But he never gets there; because his planning is always based upon today's prices and they keep going upward.

Inflation is mass confusion.

No one knows what he's doing. And every man thinks it's *he* who's out of step with the general prosperity.

The businessman, seeing his sales volume larger than ever before, wonders why he isn't showing a profit. It's all he can do to keep his business propped up with bank credit. When he confides in his banker that he thinks he may be a failure, the banker reassures him and grants him a new loan.

The consumer wonders why everyone else is doing so well. He hopes that others won't see how badly he's doing behind the façade of a prosperity he's created.

If only he could stand back from his own life, view the entire economy and see what's happening, he'd be able to reassure himself of his own sanity. And he'd be able to begin taking steps to get out of his predicament.

It's also true that whenever an individual begins to allow for inflation in his calculation, inflation speeds up and manages to stay out in front of him.

But if the next one were to be around $150? Ah, that's a different story. "Now I'm *really* getting ahead," he thinks.

It's not that the money managers are consciously aiming to throw our Dagwood Bumstead a curve. They just look at the business trends and become aware of the need for bigger and bigger doses of inflation.

So the subsidy programs get bigger and the bank credit expansion gets more feverish. But, as always, reactions are taking place that weren't anticipated.

For example, the government suffers from having to pay higher prices than expected, just as everyone does. Just like us, it plans *its* budget with today's prices in mind; but inflation is pushing those prices upward. So it, too, runs to the bank and borrows to meet a higher-than-expected deficit.

But the paper money won't be there to buy the government's bonds unless the reins on inflation are loosened a little more. So one feeds on the other and vice versa.

At the same time, individuals notice the paper money depreciating rapidly, and they become afraid to hold it. They try to spend it faster. Less savings are available for real credit, creating pressure for phony credit.

And when savings accounts go down, interest rates go up. The government tries to push the rates down by feeding more paper money into the system, hoping to make money more "plentiful."

What we're seeing here are the ways in which fires of inflation are fanned: (1) bigger spending programs are needed to keep the "boom" from collapsing; (2) unexpectedly higher prices cause the government to borrow more, requiring more inflation to make it possible; and (3) savings accounts become less attractive and consumers spend more; so more inflation appears to be the only way to hold interest rates down.

Each of these things encourages the expansion of inflation at an ever-increasing rate. It multiplies; it doesn't add. One thing feeds another; and it becomes harder and harder to hold it in check.

When it gets going fast enough, you have *runaway inflation.* (or *hyper-inflation*)-where the paper money is depreciating hourly. And within a short period of time, the entire monetary system collapses.

History is riddled with examples of runaway inflation. It reached such a critical stage during the French Revolution that the state decreed violations of its legal tender law to be guillotine offenses. Yet people *still* refused to accept the worthless currency.*

In 1923, Germans were paying a billion marks for a

*An excellent case history of runaway inflation is provided in Andrew Dickson White's Fiat *Money Inflation in France.*

for a loaf of bread. And there was China at the end of the Second World War-and Brazil and Holland and Indonesia and on and on and on.

Naturally, in each case, the cry before the crisis was "You never had it so good!"

As Ludwig von Mises has pointed out, the government is the only agency that can take a useful commodity like paper, slap some ink on it, and make it totally worthless.

POISON OR HANGING?

Somewhere in this fool's paradise, the money managers reach a critical fork in the road. After having inflated steadily, they reach a point where all the many alternatives that were once available have disappeared. There are only two dismal alternatives left.

One choice is to continue inflating. But by this point, it's gone too far. Further inflation means they'll lose control completely and runaway inflation will take over.

But the only alternative is to stop inflation. And that will bring to light all the miscalculations of the past. It means an embarrassing liquidation period ahead. Only it won't be just a recession. Now inflation has gone so far that the readjustment period will be a full-scale depression, with widespread business failures, unemployment, and bank closings.

In fact, at this point, it doesn't require a deflation (removal of paper money from circulation) in order to cause a recession. It doesn't even require an end to currency expansion. *Just slow down the rate of increase* and you bring on the depression.

So this is their choice now: runaway inflation or depression. The money managers may not even be aware that they've arrived at that juncture. They may go right on inflating, unaware of the consequences. But once they've reached that fork in the road, it's far too late to turn back and correct their mistakes.

THE GOLD RUSH

While all this is going on, the money managers are also fighting on another front.

Inflation makes many people jittery about the future of the currency. And so those who can turn their dollars for gold (mainly foreign banks and governments) do so, as they see the value of the dollar rapidly sliding downward.

The gap between the gold supply and the money substitute volume reaches a point where a run on the gold seem inevitable. And no one likes to be last in line at a run.

Preserving the remaining gold becomes a national problem. Such things as "balance of payments" become important issues. Attempts are made to keep American citizens from enhancing their lives by buying attractive foreign goods. Controls are often imposed that discourage, or totally prohibit, the sending of money to foreign countries.

It's interesting to note that, without inflation, there'd never be any such thing as a "balance of payments" problem. Every dollar that could be spent (and eventually turned into the Treasury) would have gold to back it up. Foreign trade would be encouraged as a way of widening our choices.

But with inflation, it's big problem. And the government watches its gold supply getting smaller and smaller, until the situation becomes desperate. Here, too, a juncture is finally reached were there are only two alternatives.

One obvious alternative is *deflation*-withdraw some of the excess paper money from circulation. That would close the gap between the gold supply and the volume of outstanding money substitutes, reducing the overwhelming demands on the gold stock.

But that means being prepared for the depression that would certainly follow. And if you wait too long to deflate, it can be too late. At that point, the run on the gold may have started. A short-term answer to the crisis is needed, and deflation wouldn't work fast enough.

The second alternative is widely understood. The government simply *defaults* on its agreement to redeem dollars with a stated amount of gold. Only it isn't called a default; it's called a *devaluation.*

The government has promised, in effect, to pay put one ounce of gold for every 35 dollars turned in at the Treasury. Surveying the situation, the government sees that outstanding claims against the gold stock are perhaps six times as great as the gold supply itself.

And perhaps it calculates that about half of those claims are in the hands of people in a position to exercise them. So the government finally decides it has no alternative but to change the rules in the middle of the game.

After having issued the dollars on the basis of a fixed rate of exchange, it now changes the rate. It says it will no longer redeem one ounce of gold for every 35 dollars turned in. Now it will pay out only *one-half ounce* for every 35 dollars. In other words, it will take 70 dollars, instead of 35, to claim one ounce.

This is a *devaluation: a repudiation of the government's promise to honor its money substitutes at the stated rate of exchange.*

It's important to recognize exactly what a devaluation is. It isn't a mere adjustment of exchange rates; it isn't a raising of the price of gold. *It is the act of defaulting on a debt.*

It's a bankrupt debtor deciding to pay off is debts at 50 cents on the dollar (or any other percentage chosen).

A 50% devaluation would mean changing the redemption rate from $35 per ounce to $70 per ounce, cutting the dollar's redemption value in half. A 67% devaluation would mean changing the redemption rate to $105 per ounce.

A 100% devaluation would mean refusing to redeem any gold at all. That's what American citizens suffered in 1933. Since then, no American has been legally permitted to own gold bullion or gold coins dated later than 1933.

When a government devalues its currency, it seems to take the pressure off its gold supply for awhile. Inevitably, this encourages more inflation; the consequences seem to have been eliminated. At least temporarily.

Before the devaluation, there are many stop-gap measures a government may invoke, attempting to delay the inevitable. Most of these involve a fake show of confidence in the future of the gold supply, hoping to dissuade foreign creditors from collecting their gold.

So the government ponders the dilemma of *deflation* or *devaluation* in trying to save its gold stock. And back on the other front, it's the dilemma of *runaway inflation* or *depression.*

Each of these problems becomes more and more aggravated, even while the government displays its most confident posture to the world. The bureaucrats and economists talk more and more about the "new age" of monetary matters, the "archaic reliance on gold," the gold speculators who are pictured as a villain, and other fictions that are intended to draw attention away from the *real* problems-the problem no one wants to end; *inflation.*

All the tricks up the government's sleeve have been tried before and have failed to avert the inevitable. But that won't stop it from trying again.

WHO WILL PROTECT YOU?

How many times have you heard a statement like this: "We could never have a great depression in this country; our government now has the power to intervene and prevent such things from happening"?

In the first chapter of this book, we saw that there was no shortage of governmental powers in 1929. Still, there was a depression. It's very instructive to review events of the 1920s and 1930s. They represent the classic example of the inflation-depression cycle we've been examining in this book.

Anyone who believes that America of the 1920's was an example of unregulated free enterprise hasn't checked history very closely. As noted before, I recommend Murray Rothbard's outstanding book, *America's Great Depression*, as the most thorough economic history of the period 1921-1933.

In Rothbard's book, I counted 43 major federal activities in operation during the "Roaring Twenties." Here are some of the programs:

1. The Federal Reserve System launched a full-scale bank inflation during the twenties. By controlling the reserve requirements, it gave banks the lending power to create new paper money. In addition, in 1923, the Reserve Banks began purchasing government bonds in the open market to facilitate deficit spending and to add to the paper money supply.

Prices could have gone down during the twenties; it was a period of high production. But it became apparent that the federal reserve Board was following a policy aimed at stabilizing prices. Later, John Maynard Keynes hailed "the successful management of the dollar by the Federal Reserve Board from 1923 to 1928...."

2. Meanwhile, the New York Federal Reserve Bank extended credit directly to the Bank of England to help offset the damage done by the British inflation (just as it did during the sixties). Similar credits were extended to the central banks of Belgium, Poland, and Italy.

3. In August 1921, Congress authorized one billion dollars in credits to the War Finance Corporation, to be lent directly to farmer's cooperatives and foreign importers of American farm goods. The purposes of the bill were to raise farm prices, provide cheap credit to farmers, and increase farm exports. There hasn't been a free market in Agriculture since then.

4. During the First World War, the government seized the railroads. They were finally returned to their owners in 1920. But in 1926, the Railway Labor Act was passed. This imposed upon the railroads the same sort of regulation that the National Labor Relations Act later brought to rest of American industry.

5. Federal taxing policies were used to influence activity in the stock market. In addition, the futures markets were regulated as a result of the Capper Grain Futures Act and the Future Trading Act.

6. Business regulation started with the signing of the Constitution and its provisions for tariffs and interstate commerce laws. But it greatly heightened by the anti-trust legislation passed at the turn of the century, plus the establishment of the Federal Trade Commission, the Interstate Commerce Commission, etc.

So please don't delude yourself by looking to the government to prevent the inevitable consequences of inflation. That's asking the problem to provide the solution.

There's never been any shortage of governmental intervention in the economy. But those who say, "We won't have a rerun of 1929 because the government has more power to intervene," are actually correct. The government *does* have more power; and so we won't have a return of 1929.

We'll have something more severe.

In general, American depressions have been getting steadily worse. As the government develops more "sophisticated" techniques for prolonging the inflationary cycles, it causes more painful liquidation periods.

INFLATION IN THE TWENTIES

The seeds of the 1929 depression were planted in the First World War and the inflation that accompanied it. After the war, some of the paper money was cleared out, causing the recession of 1921.

Then the state embarked upon a full-scale inflationary cycle lasting through 1928, at which point money substitutes outnumbered the real money by a ratio of eight to one.

PAPER MONEY SUPPLY

(December 31, 1928)

Checking Account Deposits:	$23.1 billion
Currency in Circulation:	3.6 billion
Total Money Substitutes:	$26.7 billion
Gold Stock (real money):	$ 3.0 billion

The big problem facing the money managers in late 1928 was the heavy demand to redeem gold, coming from both Americans and foreigners. The federal Reserve Board chose to meet the issue by deflation, rather than by devaluation. The inflationary cycle ended and the inevitable miscalculations started coming to light.

THE STOCK MARKET

It's important to realize that the stock market, like everything else in the economy, displays the effects of inflation. In fact, it's a particularly sensitive indicator of paper money in circulation because of its liquidity. Its constantly changing price structure.

The stock market not only responds to inflation, it also benefits from it. It's like the swimming pool industry. It's an ideal investment receptacle for people who've been led to believe they have the more money than they really do. On an inflationary cycle, many people who have no business investing think they have the funds to do so.

This pushes stock prices up faster than the general price rise. Other people, viewing the stock market from outside, see it as a way to beat the depreciation of the dollar. They withdraw their savings from banks and buy stocks instead.

The availability of margin credit adds to the number of people better on higher stock prices. But margin credit isn't the culprit of the stock market orgies. The villain is inflation. Without inflation, there wouldn't be the feeling that higher prices are inevitable. People wouldn't be so anxious to use margin if they thought there was a good chance the stock price might drop; for losses are greater if the falling stock is margined.

In addition, the paper money needed for margin loans wouldn't be available without inflation.

The new paper money flowing into the stock market bids the prices of stocks well beyond the levels justified by any prosperity the companies involved are experiencing. So we see stocks selling at 30 to 100 times their earning values.

At that point, the stock market moves by *psychology* rather than fundamentals. It's no longer a question of what particular *company* is likely to do in the future. The question is: what will *other speculators* think the stock of the company will do?

Chartists take over the market, looking for statistical trends, "break-outs," and other phenomena of *mass psychology*. The real fundamentals are ignored: supply and demand, company profits, markets, managements, etc.

But when the inflation ends, the stock market begins to drop-*inevitably*. It *has* to drop because there's no longer enough paper money to support the higher price level.

All during 1929, people in the stock market fought to push the market to higher levels. They succeeded temporarily, despite the deflation beginning around them. But the break had to come. By October, the point had been reached where it was literally impossible to support the old price levels; the paper money just didn't exist anymore.

The panic on October 29 wasn't the cause of the depression, nor even the beginning of it. It was simply the irrefutable signal that there was a depression in progress-that the dream world had ended. The price was about to be paid for years of tinkering with the paper money supply.

All speculative orgies are the result of inflation. Neither stock booms nor land booms could be sustained without inflation. There just aren't the resources available for people to buy-at-any-price unless inflation is pouring paper money into the economy. And the boom always collapses when the inflation ends.

THE DEPRESSION BEGINS

Surprisingly, once the inflationary cycle ends, there doesn't have to be widespread misery. The greatest losers will be the businessmen who have large sums of capital tied up in production facilities and inventories that aren't needed.

With the inflation over, prices and wages will drop to whatever realistic points are required to get things moving again. Unwanted inventories will move at *some* price; and workers can be employed at *some* wage. No matter what the state of the economy, there are an infinite number of unsatisfied human desires; thus, there's always a market for someone to work to satisfy them.

But what distinguishes a painful depression from a mild recession is the inability to get it over with. If the government has enough control over the economy, it usually will use that power to *prevent* wages and prices from falling to their natural levels. For some strange reason, high prices and high wages are assumed to be symptoms of a healthy economy-whereas they are only symptoms of inflation.

And so everything is done to hold the price level u, even though it isn't possible to trade at those higher prices. And, in the process, the economy comes to a dead stop. You can't have a world of high price levels when then the paper money needed to support those levels is no longer there.

The 1929 depression evoked the ultimate in governmental interference. Herbert Hoover has been characterized so as a "do nothing" President and the symbol of the "rugged individualist." But that isn't true. He reacted to the depression by calling for a fantastic program to keep wages and prices high, and to prevent the liquidation of mistakes.

He vows to reverse all previous governmental policies in fighting this depression. And he did. In the process, he succeeded in keeping the economy immobilized.

When Franklin Roosevelt ran against Hoover in 1932, he castigated the President for his big-government techniques. He promised to cut the size of government and to let free enterprise make its way out of depression unhampered.

Naturally, that never happened. Politicians only call for the reduction of powers they don't hold themselves. Governors, in general, are for states' "rights." President are for federal "rights." If you want to change a governor's attitude toward federal power, make him President.

Roosevelt decided on a different policy from that pursued by Hoover, however. He was anxious to get the engine of inflation going again. But there was still that strain on the gold stock.

So he removed the pressure by prohibiting Americans from owning gold (a 100% devaluation), and then devalued the dollar by 41% for foreigners.

This gave him clear sailing to inflate with a vengeance. And he did.

But he continued to force wage and price levels as high as possible, and they managed to stay ahead of the inflationary push. So nothing happened. At the end of the thirties, there was still no improvement. And by that time, the economy was tied up in red tape.

Finally, the preparation for war created an all-out inflation that broke the price-fixing logjam, and things began to move.

Since then, we've been on one long inflationary spree. Each attempt to slow down the cycle has been met with a recession and quick return to more inflation. The mistakes being piled up are enormous; and the problem has reached far greater dimensions than those that existed in 1929.

The next time you read that we're in the longest sustained "boom" in American history, you must remind yourself that, unfortunately, this means we're awaiting the worst depression yet.

The boom is unreal; but that doesn't mean that all the prosperity is. America's great productive strength has grown steadily since the industrial revolution. It's the growth in technical proficiency that has brought us prosperity. That growth is the only meaningful kind of progress in the real world. To whatever extent there is inflation, to that extent the prosperity is *diminished*.

How can one believe that the hundreds of billions of dollars spent on wars and foreign aid and welfare can possibly produce prosperity? That capital and energy and time could have gone into building things that actually improved out standard of living. Instead the resources have been diverted into non-productive enterprises that reduced what we've have had otherwise.

It staggers the mind to wonder what we'd be enjoying today if we hadn't lost so much of our productivity to wasteful endeavors encouraged by the inflationary cycle.

How far has that cycle gone? Here is the scorecard:

PAPER MONEY SUPPLY:

(December 30, 1970)

Checking Account Deposits:	$211.1 billion
Currency in Circulation:	48.9 billion
Total Money Substitutes:	260.0 billion
Gold Stock (real money):	$11.1 billion

The inflationary ratio was eight to one in 1928. Now it's 25 to one. The money substitutes are 25 times the gold stock backing them up.

These are mere figures and I know of no magic formula that attaches any particular significance to any particular ratio. But we can see that since 1966 the ratio has changed its direction, when plotted on a graph (see next page). Even the slight decrease in the ratio in 1970 was due more than anything else to a slight increase in the gold supply.

WILL THE GOVERNMENT SAVE US?

We still hear over and over again that there could never be another depression because the government has the power to prevent it. But how can the government prevent it? In the first place, as we've seen, the government is the problem.

Depressions aren't caused by stock market speculation, by unregulated free enterprise, by gold speculators, by greedy profiteers, by shortages of demand, by capitalism, nor by lack of confidence. Depressions are caused by the government's inflationary printing of paper money.

Secondly, even if the government did have the power to stop a depression, how could anyone be willing to put his faith in the government's ability to use it wisely?

This is the same government that has promised since 1964 to put and early end to the Vietnam war. This is the government that solved our financial problems by removing the gold reserve requirements for paper money and bank deposits.

This is the government that today, while the economy is already dizzy from deficit spending, is toying with more ambitious programs for outer space and free medical care for everyone.

Even if the government did have the power to prevent depressions, who could believe that every one of the two million bureaucrats who have anything to do with the problem will handle his role wisely? Is that where you want to put your faith?

How does the government plan to deal with runaway inflation? No one has suggested putting an end to the inflationary printing of paper money. Instead, all the discussions revolve around wage and price controls. That will just make matters worse. There's no way to control *every* wage and price. So, with real inflation continuing unchecked, the prices of all *un*controlled products and services will continue to go up.

That makes it unprofitable for individuals whose income is controlled to continue selling their products and services at the controlled prices. So they quit producing and tremendous shortages result.

And I'm sure that while that's happening, there'll be plenty of spokesmen to tell us how capably the government can control the economy.

The fact is the government *can't* control the economy. Such a thing is literal impossibility. Whenever it tries, it only makes matters worse. There's no way the government can repeal the natural law that you'll only produce or exchange when you believe it will lead to something you want. And yet, every governmental economic rule is an attempt to repeal that law-so every interference with the market fails to fulfill the "noble" purpose that was intended.

Some people believe that an end to the war in Vietnam would save the economy. I don't. It's true that giving those billions of war dollars back to the people to spend for themselves would help considerably-but even that wouldn't be enough to reverse history of the past thirty years.

And it's foolish to think that the money actually would be returned to the people in the form of tax relief or an end to deficit spending. It's almost inevitable that the money would be kept in Washington to be spent on every conceivable scheme the frustrated politicians can dream up.

Big government always goes on unchecked. The end of the Korean war had no effect whatsoever upon the growth of government. Neither will an end to the war on Vietnam-if and when that ever happens.

And don't be naïve enough to think that a change of administration would make any difference. Since the first world war, not one president has done anything to reverse the trend. Each one has been a slave to the merry-go-round he inherited.

So how could we possibly believe governments will be our salvation? It's the government that put us in this mess-and it's the government that aggravates it daily.

Economic cycles are a fact of life. And they'll continue to be so-as long as most people believe governments are capable of doing for them what they're unwilling to do for themselves.

And we're rapidly approaching the crisis point of this economic cycle. There's no way it can be prevented-although it may be delayed and aggravated by further government schemes. But there's no way the clichés we continually hear can solve the problem.

We're told what we need is confidence. But confidence in what? Confidence that the immutable laws of economics have been repealed? Confidence that the world is going to start spinning in the opposite direction from now on? Confidence that acts no longer have consequences?

Can a man falling from a 30-story window, pulled toward the ground by gravity, solve his problem with confidence?

We're told that we don't need gold. "After all, the dollar is backed by the tremendous productive capacity of the nation." That has a nice ring to it-until you examine it a little more closely. For what's being said is that the government apparently has the right to confiscate *your* production to back up *its* currency.

The currency and the economy are two different things. The government is wholly responsible for the currency it issues. We, as individual human beings, are responsible for our own productivity. If you'd like to pledge your wealth, your resources, and your production as the backing for the government's currency, you're welcome to. But I find the idea less than appealing.

Money is a commodity that's accepted in exchange. It's not a hope, not an abstraction, not a measure of production, not a short-term note. It's a commodity that individual human beings are willing to hold while waiting to make purchases.

No one will produce or exchange unless he believes it will lead ultimately to something he wants.

You can't impose a valueless money system upon people and expect that there won't be reactions. Gold and silver evolved as money commodities out of billions and billions of human exchanges. They won't be superseded within our lifetimes. Governments can reject them, but individuals will continue to use them.

That won't stop government officials from looking for ways to replace gold, however. But there is no way out of their dilemma. Special Drawing Rights ("paper gold") aren't the answer. World currencies aren't the answer. There isn't any answer, because the money managers don't even understand the question.

Governments don't like gold because it tells them when they do wrong things. Without the gold, they might be able to stretch their misdeeds a little further.

But it won't stop the consequences. They're inevitable.

You can't build a monetary system on sand and expect anything but dire consequences.

And that's exactly what we have today-a system that's based upon a commodity with no inherent value.

ADVANTAGES OF GOLD & SILVER AS MONEY:	ADVANTAGES OF PAPER AS MONEY:
1. Durable	1.
2. Divisible	2.
3. Convenient	3.
4. Consistent	4.
5. Accepted Value	5.

ADVISORY 5

"Floating Currencies"

Another of the many currency misconceptions has to do with the free market rates of currency exchange.

If a government were to play the game honestly (meaning that it would redeem gold for its currency to anyone who asked for it), the free market rate of exchange for that currency would be relatively stable. No one would pay more for the currency (not sell if for less) than its basic rate; for it would be more advantageous to deal directly with the treasury of the government itself.

In practice, however, few governments deal honestly with their currencies. They issue far more paper money than they can back with gold-and this leads them to impose various kinds of restrictions upon the ways that individuals can deal with their currencies.

As a result, the currencies fluctuate in value in the free market as some look weaker than others. (In truth, no currencies ever really get stronger; it only becomes stronger relative to other currencies that are weakening faster.)

The impractical concept of "western solidarity" has led to the agreement among western governments that they'd help support each other's currencies in the free market. What it means is this: if one currency becomes too weak relative to another currency, the government of the stronger currency agrees to go into the free market and use its currency to purchase the weaker currency.

This is supposed to do two things: (1) At the time of the purchase, it helps to push the currency price back to its "official" level; and (2) the commitment to do this is supposed to discourage private speculation in currencies-since the currency apparently will never vary much in price.

As with any other governmental currency policy, this simply encourages most governments to be more reckless in their fiscal matters-since they expect other governments to bail them out when trouble starts.

Eventually, of course, the most frugal governments become fed up and refuse to issue more of their currency. After all, what they're getting in return for it is a weak currency with very little gold backing.

The Canadian government withdrew from the game in June, 1970, and the German government did the same in May, 1971. Each government refused to continue issuing more of its currency for the purpose of propping up the price of the American dollar in international exchange.

What these governments did wasn't a devaluation or an upvaluation. In each case, gold redemption values of all currencies involved remained unchanged. But it did mean that their currencies' prices would float freely in the marketplace relative to the dollar.

UPVALUATIONS

A government that has agreed to buy up weak dollars has a second alternative available too it-different from that chosen by the Canadian and German governments. It can do what the Swiss government did in May, 1971.

It continued its agreement to receive dollars-but raised the price by 7.07%. It now pays out fewer Swiss francs for each dollar received. It did this by raising the gold content of the Swiss franc.

This is an *upvaluation* or *revaluation*-which is the opposite of a devaluation. Instead of changing the rules to cheat its creditors, it changed the rules so that holders of its currency can receive *more* gold than had been promised previously.

I presume the Swiss government did this so it could continue honoring its agreement to accept dollars, but hoping that the higher price of Swiss francs would discourage the inflow of dollars. I personally think it was a mistake on the part of the Swiss government; for it means they're paying for someone else's mistakes. I believe the course of action taken by the Canadian and German governments was more realistic. (The German government had taken the upvaluation route in October, 1969, and may have decided that it was too costly.)

Upvaluations are harmful to anyone who's holding dollars but who must deal in the upvalued currency. Conversely, an upvaluation is beneficial to anyone holding the upvalued currency.

The upvaluation of the Swiss franc in 1971 may have been a blessing in disguise to American investors who had put off protecting themselves by changing their dollars for francs. It should have pointed up the gravity of the situation-while, at the same time, the small 7% upvaluation wasn't enough to make it no longer worthwhile to switch into Swiss francs.

Eventually, the U.S. government may prohibit its citizens from sending dollars overseas-so the time to do it is now.

THE COMING CRISIS

It's obvious, in 1971, that the crisis has already begun. But there is most likely will be lulls and storms alternating until it gets much worse.

Finally, the more frugal governments will have to refuse to continue supporting the dollar. (I'm sure they'll be many Americans who'll call it "ingratitude"-but it will happen anyways.)

The dollar will become progressively weaker. Finally, the U.S. government may put an "embargo" on gold. It would be referred to as "an end to the *selling* of gold for the benefit of greedy speculators and uncooperative foreign governments." But the U.S. doesn't *sell* gold; it's simply redeeming with gold the billions of IOU's it's issued.

Such an "embargo" is really a 100% devaluation-reducing the gold content of the dollar to zero.

This would either put an immediate end to foreign trade or, at least, cause the value of the dollar to nosedive. Foreigners would be unable to get much value for the dollars they receive; in fact, they'd probably have to exchange dollars on the black market for very little in return.

Before all this happen, there may be various kinds of new agreements worked out between the governments involved to try to forestall the final crash, but that will only delay things temporarily.

The only way the final crash of the dollar could be avoided would be for the American government to deflate its currency and accept the inevitable depression that has to come. Unfortunately, I find it hard to conceive of any politician doing this.

More likely then, we can expect a devaluation of the dollar in the range of 50%-67%-or even the possibility of the total destruction of the dollar through runaway inflation.

REPLACEMENT OF THE CURRENCY

Many people apparently think a devaluation means the currency will be replaced with a new currency. This has often happened during runaway inflation periods in other countries.

The purpose is merely to make exchange more convenient, however. The government issues a new dollar, worth (for example) 100 of the old dollars. All prices naturally readjust in the marketplace to the new currency.

Such an event is not a devaluation, however.

I have no idea whether or not it will happen. Since a replacement in currency doesn't ordinarily involve any substantial change in the total value of your holdings, there's no reason to make any special attempt to hedge against it.

THE BLAME

During any crisis, the U.S. government inevitably will blame "uncooperative" foreign governments and "greedy" speculators.

But, as usual, it'll be pointing the finger at the *effects* of the crisis, not the *cause*. The problem has been caused by the U.S. government's overprinting of paper money and the pouring of that money overseas in foreign aid and military commitments.

There's never been any "balance of payments" problem insofar as private trade has been concerned. The imbalance has been the result of the government's attempts to police the world and to bring prosperity to everyone. It's obvious that there's no point in arguing over whether or not the government *should* help the world; the truth is that the U.S. government *can't* help the world.

All of these problems can be traced to the government's simple little decision to inflate the currency a wee bit-way back many generations ago. Who would have believed that such a tiny little transgression could grow and grow-like a malignant tumor-until it finally erupted into the cancer of today's currency crisis?

WHEN?

There's no way to foretell the exact timing of devaluation. It can come about as a cool, calculated political decision. Or a government can do it in desperation, under pressure for a run on its gold.

One point should be emphasized: don't pay any attention to statements by bureaucrats. They are totally meaningless. As former Defense Department official Arthur Sylvester pointed out, government officials feel justified in lying to preserve their own positions.

Henry Hazlitt, in his fine book *What You Should Know About Inflation*, has called attention to the classic example of bureaucratic fraudulence.

He cites a series of nine different statements made by Sir Stafford Cripps, then Chancellor of the Exchequer, denying that the British pound would be devalued.

These occurred between January 26, 1948, and September 6, 1949. They included such remarks as: "A reported plan to devalue the pound is complete nonsense"; "there will be no devaluation of the pound sterling"; "devaluation is neither advisable nor even possible"; "no one need fear devaluation of our currency in any circumstances"; etc.

Can you guess what happened on September 18, 1949?

Yes, the pound was devalued.

This isn't an exceptional example. Money managers fear advance warning of a devaluation. They'll deny it down to Friday night at midnight; and then devalue on Saturday morning.

And that's another point. Devaluations take place on weekends when the markets are closed. They come by surprise, whenever possible. So don't wait for a bill to be introduced in Congress before preparing for a devaluation. There won't be any bill.

The Cripps story is cited to warn you not to pay the slightest attention to any statements made by bureaucrats regarding the possibility of devaluation. In fact, after the devaluation took place, Cripps defended his record of denials by saying, "No responsible minister could possibly have done otherwise than deny such intention."

Whether or not you agree with him, recognize that this is the way governments operate.

However, as already mentioned, the decision may not be made with cool, deliberate forethought. It may be forced on the government in the heat of a run on the gold.

In that case, you'll have some warning during the preceding week; but that's the worst time to hedge against a devaluation. The price of every hedge is shooting upward as other people are also trying to protect themselves.

If you buy your hedge then, you'll be paying a high price. And if the devaluation *doesn't* happen that weekend, the price of the hedge will drop again the following week.

So, by waiting until the last minute, you're putting yourself in a very difficult position.

Because its only alternative is deflation, *a devaluation is an overwhelming probability.* It's hard to believe that Richard Nixon would be willing to assume the Herbert Hoover image. It isn't that a devaluation will solve the inflation-caused problems; it's just that politicians generally *think* it will.

Since we live in an uncertain world, where *all* relevant factors can never be known, it would be foolish of me to make a prediction as to either *when* or even *if.*

Instead, let me say, that I *expect* a devaluation to occur sometime between this coming Saturday and the end of 1971. I'll be surprised (but not shocked) if it doesn't.

In the next section, we'll take a brief look at business decisions, with respect to the possibilities we've been examining.

Then we'll go into the details of devaluation's effect upon every major kind of investment. We'll also see how each of these investments would be affected by runaway inflation, a short-term recession, a depression, or continued inflation.

It will be apparent that many popular hedges against these possibilities are *not* really hedges at all.

THE EFFECTS

UPON YOUR BUSINESS

It's very easy to develop a "split personality" about some things in life. You read a book like this, concern yourself with the investments you're making and how they'll be affected by the possibilities we've been examining. Then you do something to make yourself less vulnerable.

And then, the next morning, you go back to your job at that multi-million-dollar swimming pool company.

But the world we live in is a single, complex entity. The events we're discussing will affect your investments, your business, even your purchases as a consumer.

Whether you own your own business or work for someone else, now is the time to take a good look at the industry in which you make your living.

The first question to ask is: How much has the industry been aided by inflation? Is the product or service involved a luxury that wouldn't have fared as well if there'd been no boom?

The industries aided most by inflation will suffer the most from a recession, depression, or devaluation. In many cases, companies will; in some cases, whole industries may be liquidated.

If you own or manage a business that's vulnerable in this way, wouldn't it be a good idea to make plans to get out of that business or a convert your operation to a less vulnerable line? Difficult as that might seem to be right now, it'll be much easier today than it will be in the next year or the year after.

If you're in a business that isn't overly vulnerable, you'll still have the basic problems of coping with the various phenomena we've see. And you should begin today to make the necessary plans to be followed, if and when any of the possibilities occur.

Even in the present national economic conditions, there are certain characteristics of continued inflation that will affect you.

As this book has been saying over and over again, confusion reigns n the inflationary economy. It will become progressively harder to make accurate calculations of future business. The normal signals of consumer demand are distorted and will get much more distorted.

You naturally expect to be able to adjust to inflation, to take it into consideration in future decisions. But, somehow, more experience doesn't help any of us interpret trends in an inflationary economy.

One of the biggest business fallacies is the idea that large sales volume creates, or leads to, large profits. Inflation always leads you to believe that your prosperity is just around the corner. "Just a few more sales and we'll be in the black." But your costs will always be more than you expected. So the truth may be that the bigger your sales volume, the bigger your losses.

Traditionally, it has always been a virtue for an entrepreneur to think in the long term. The man who could engineer long-term plans could gain the greatest rewards in the market. But in an inflation, the very opposite is the case.

The longer the time span of your production or marketing plans, the more vulnerable you are to a host of unpleasant possibilities that didn't exist when you made the plan. Also, if inflation has caused you to miscalculate, you'll have lost that much more before discovering the miscalculations.

So you should be looking for ways to deal more in the short term, with less dependence upon the far-off uncertain future.

This also means you should arrange marketing programs and production plans with as much *flexibility* as possible. Put yourself in a position where you aren't overly committed to a plan that could go sour because you hadn't calculated correctly.

If you haven't already done so, reread earlier chapters with your business or occupation in mind. Try to determine your vulnerability to each set of possibilities we've investigated. List them; and then set about eliminating as many as possible.

One way to eliminate vulnerability is to decentralize. Liquidate as much of your physical equipment as you can; then lease on relatively short-term contracts.

Whenever possible, eliminate employees from your payroll. Replace them by contracting for the services needed, either with individuals or businesses. In many cases, your former employee will be the new contractor. But your new arrangement will be far more flexible than the old one was; and invariably it will cost less.

Above all, recognize what's been stated earlier-that the government has a bad habit of changing the rules in the middle of the game. Don't treat the present legal structure as a permanent condition. Laws change daily-inevitably toward greater governmental intervention.

Business frequently lay out long-range plans that never reach fruition because they're thwarted by new government regulations. Always ask yourself, "What am I making myself vulnerable to? What kinds of new regulations could hurt me?"

Arrange everything with maximum flexibility in mind. Don't put yourself out on a limb where the bureaucracy will saw you off.

The government is a fact of life; and it'll become a larger and larger consideration in your business as time passes. But if you stay flexible and alert to loopholes, you can minimize its interference and continue to profit.

Of course, there's the alternative of thinking that you personally will be able to change the government's plan and change the course of history.

ADVISORY 6

The Balance Sheet

We've covered a lot of ground since we embarked on Chapter 1 to have a look at the nature of the monetary crisis.

To be sure we haven't skipped anything important, let's summarize the principal characteristics of each of the possibilities, and see which investments respond in the best way to each of the possibilities.

CONTINUED INFLATION

There's no way to foretell how much longer the present inflationary cycle can continue. But we do know that the longer it lasts, the more hectic it will be. There'll be more-frequent "quickie" recessions, followed by renewed inflation.

This means more confusion, more difficulty making rational business, financial, and personal economic decisions. A farsighted individual will use this period to get his house in order, eliminate his vulnerabilities, and create the framework by which he can profit from the coming events.

Here are the 18 investments, classified by the ways that continued inflation will affect them:

Very good: Diamonds, art objects, etc., stocks and mutual funds.

Good: Cash (for liquidity), commodities (but risky for amateur), gold bullion, gold coins, gold stocks, income real estate, undeveloped land, silver bullion, silver coins, silver stocks.

Break-even: Bonds, life insurance, mortgages, residential real estate, Swiss francs.

Bad: Short selling.

RECESSION

The absence of a drop in the general price level is the most significant feature of contemporary short-term recessions. At the same time, however, there'll be considerable drops in the prices and liquidity of inflation-inspired items.

Good: Gold stocks, short selling.

Break-even: Bonds, cash, gold bullion, life insurance, mortgages, Swiss francs.

Bad: Commodities, diamonds, art objects, gold coins, income real estate, undeveloped land, residential real estate, silver bullion, silver coins, silver stocks, other stocks and mutual funds.

DEPRESSION

All indications are that the next depression will be more severe than the last one was. The politicians have managed to make the current inflationary cycle last longer than any previous one.

Therefore, the liquidation period will be even more difficult than the 1929 readjustment. And greater governmental interference will make the next depression mush stickier. You should be prepared for everything that happened before-and for things that may be much worse.

This means that some of the investments indicated below as attractive may also be vulnerable to government intervention.

Very good: Bonds, cash (outside of banks), short selling.

Good: Gold stocks, life insurance, silver bullion, silver coins, silver stocks.

Break-even: Swiss francs (safety).

Uncertain: Gold bullion, gold coins.

Bad: Mortgages.

Very Bad: Commodities, diamonds, art objects, income real estate, undeveloped land, residential real estate, stocks and mutual funds.

RUNAWAY INFLATION

This is the worst possible thing that can happen. If it does happen, you want to be as far as possible from metropolitan areas. And you'll need to be well stocked with what you need to survive, including silver coins for trading purposes.

Very good: Gold bullion, gold coins, gold stocks (not in the country where runaway inflation occurs), silver coins.

Good: Silver bullion, silver stocks (see gold stocks above), Swiss francs.

Very bad: Commodities, diamonds, art objects, income real estate, land, mortgages, residential real estate (in cities), short selling, stocks and mutual funds.

Worthless: Bonds, cash, life insurance.

DEVALUATION

If after the devaluation the number of dollars spent for imports is as big or bigger than it was previously, a deflation-like atmosphere will set in. There's better than a 50% probability that this will happen.

Exports will flourish until renewed inflation at home cuts into profits. Imports will be hurt.

Any asset you hold in an international market, where the price is measured in dollars, will give you a profit from devaluation. Immediately after the devaluation, you can convert it to more dollars than you originally spent for the asset. But some assets will profit far more than others.

Expect inflation to be renewed with vigor after the devaluation.

Very Good: Gold bullion, gold coins, gold stocks, short selling, silver bullion, silver coins, silver stocks, Swiss francs.

Good: Diamonds, art objects.

Break-even: Bonds, cash, life insurance, mortgages, residential real estate.

Bad: Commodities, income real estate, land, stocks, and mutual funds.

On the next page you'll find a summary of all the investments we've examined.

The quick review in this chapter was intended as a summary of the material we've already covered. Please don't act upon any of these recommendations without consulting the more detailed explanations given in previous chapters.

Understand, also, that these are only my best estimates of what's most likely to happen in each cases. No one can foretell with certainty all of the possible conditions that might affect any of these investments.

Now we're ready to put all of this together into an investment program that will protect you (and provide a profit) no matter which way the economy goes.

ADVISORY 7

The Investment Program

We live in an uncertain world. No one can hope to gather all the information necessary to predict with certainty the timing of specific events.

But this doesn't stop us from seeing the broad picture of what is to come. We know that certain acts produce certain consequences. Since those acts have already taken place, it's just a matter of time now until consequences take place.

As I wrote this book, the thought kept nagging at me: "I hope it doesn't reach the market too late!" And yet, it may prove to have been published two years earlier than necessary. If so, it's far better to be ready two years too early, rather than *one day* to late.

It's been mentioned already that *there are no precedents* to guide us in certain areas. For example, there's never been an all-out runaway inflation in this nation. As a result, we can only use logic to project the conditions that would prevail.

There are similar historical vacancies about technical reactions of gold stocks, free market bullion prices, etc., to a devaluation.

The scientific method is a four-step process: (1) *observe* the world around you; (2) *draw conclusions* concerning cause-and-effect relationships; (3) *make tests* to see if you can accurately predict results: and (4) *refine your principles* through continued observations and tests.

Where we have no precedents to guide us, we're limited to the first two steps. There's no way we can *test* our conclusions until the one all-important moment comes.

We can only observe the world around us, draw conclusions (PAGE MISSING pages 171 and 172)

But will give you safety: it is, in effect, an insurance policy. In the same way, the Swiss franc savings account won't provide a profit (the interest on the account will permit you to break even with inflation). But it will provide important liquidity for any possibility to come.

The bulk of your investment capital will be profit-making areas, however. The silver bullion should appreciate in value and the gold stocks, if selected carefully, should profit from the rising free-market price of gold.

The silver coins will increase in price along with the silver bullion, so you'll be showing a profit there.

The retreat won't show a profit. But if you select it to be an attractive vacation spot, it will pay its way regardless. Make it as comfortable a hideaway as possible; so that you'll enjoy being there during good times.

Your total capital should increase fairly substantially within 18 months from the implementation of this program.

Short-term recessions: This is the only possibility in which you'll show a loss; but there are very few good investments for a recession. We've intentionally sacrificed this possibility because it's the least critical. Whichever was the economy goes from there, you'll be well covered.

In the event of a recession, you'll break even on the cash and the Swiss francs. The gold stocks may appreciate, but your silver bullion and coins will probably depreciate slightly. The retreat won't be affected one way or the other; it won't be necessary yet.

Depression: If a full-scale depression occurs, the cash will continue to be valuable because of its safest from bank runs. The Swiss franc savings account will provide the liquid funds with which to buy, at bargain prices, the things that will comprise the foundation of your new future.

The silver bullion and coins should profit, for reasons covered in an earlier chapter. Gold stocks will most likely appreciate greatly. The retreat will be haven of safety if civil disorder should accompany the depression.

Your investments will probably grow in value during the depression. In addition, you'll have the cash with which to buy many other things that will grow in value later, as things begin to return to normal.

Runaway Inflation: If this happens, the silver coins will enable you to survive the runaway period, and to trade with others afterward. You should be at your retreat; the city will be no place in which to live at a time like this.

When you see retail prices starting to move every other day or so, spend your cash for anything you need (just get rid of it usefully). Dispose of any American gold stocks you're holding (and possibly your South African stocks, too); convert the proceeds into silver coins and head for your retreat. You'll pay a big premium for the coins at that point, but they'll be more valuable than worthless paper.

Leave the Swiss francs and the silver bullion in your Swiss account. They'll be worth a great deal to you when the crisis is over. In the meantime, your retreat should be well stocked so that, with the silver coins, you can last a year if you have to.

Devaluation: When the devaluation happens, you'll score very well. Your gold stocks may be worth several times their former value. As indicated before, sell them at the first post-devaluation peak-unless it appears the devaluation was too small and another will follow.

The silver bullion will at least double in value (given a 50% devaluation). If you decide to use leverage, your profits may be even bigger. You may want to take your profits immediately after the devaluation, waiting to see which way the price of silver will go then. The coins will have been purchased on a cash basis, so they profit to the extent of devaluation.

The Swiss francs will also profit to the extent of the devaluation. After it's over, convert them back to dollars-just in case the Swiss franc should be devalued in the aftermath.

While these four assets will be increasing in value, prices will remain relatively stable here for the near term.

You may want to bring some of your profits home and spend them while you can still do so.

The retreat won't be affected by the devaluation; neither will the small amount of cash your holding.

SUMMARY

The only eventuality that won't provide a profit for you will be the short-term recession, and it should be just that-short-term. As long as you have some liquidity, there's nothing to do but simply wait it out.

In the event of a depression, some of your investments will show a profit, and the Swiss francs will give you buying power at the most opportune time. And in a runaway inflation, you'll not only have precious safety, but assets that will be appreciating and providing the basis for new wealth in the aftermath.

A devaluation will compound your capital several times over on one Saturday morning. And even if nothing happens, during a continuation of the *status quo*, your investments will appreciate-and you'll be able to sleep nights, even amid the chaos around you.

ADVISORY 8

Precious Metals Described

DEVOLOPING YOUR STRATEGY

Owning physical gold, silver, and platinum has long been considered a vitally important method of protecting your wealth in an extremely volatile economic climate. Taking the strategic steps necessary to preserve your wealth may be as important right now as it has ever been.

Developing a well-planed diversification strategy is the first step. It provides you with a secure and trusted method for moving a portion of your money from declining paper currencies into the right precious metals over the long term.

Whether your objective is to hedge against potential inflation, safeguard assets from stock market volatility, protect yourself from further declines in the value of the U.S. dollar or simply add precious metals to your retirement portfolio. There are a number of ways to take advantage of the gold, silver, and platinum markets that many experts feel are only starting to show their true potential.

OWING THE BEST OF THE BEST

There are companies that specialize in gold, silver and platinum coins produced by the United States mint. These coins are in our vault collection also enjoy the full backing of the U.S. government for their content, weight and purity. In addition, our U.S. government issued coins are authorized by Congress and struck with "face value" denominations, making them official U.S. legal tender.

The two main sectors of precious metals we deal with are certified and bullion coins. A certified, or graded, coin is one that has undergone careful scrutiny be an independent coin-grading service in order to determine the coin's overall condition. A certified coin's grade is important because the grade determines the population of a given type of coin and therefore, its potential rarity. In other words, a certified coin holds not only market value in actual gold weight, but also numismatic (collectible) value.

On the other hand, bullion is a non-certified coin with its market value based primarily on its weight in gold and the current market price. Yet its liquidity and intrinsic value make it an important part of any precious metals portfolio.

SHORT-TERM GROWTH

Diversifying for the short term simply means integrating non-certified gold bullion into your precious metals portfolio. Bullion is unlike rare and collectible coins that have been examined and graded by a professional grading service. As mentioned earlier, a bullion's coin market value is tied primarily with its weight in gold and current market price, making it a more liquid, short-term hold. As the chart on the right shows, we recommend allocating approximately 30% of your precious metals portfolio to the gold bullion sector.

LONG-TERM GROWTH

Even more important than our short-term growth strategy is our strong belief in diversifying different percentages of the U.S. government-issued certified gold, silver and platinum coins that support long-term growth.

High-grade precious metals are an essential piece of any portfolio. With certified coins, you have the opportunity for greater protection from the market fluctuations. Furthermore, diversifying within the certified coin sector itself allows you to implement a second barrier of security-the numismatic value of the coin. That's why its recommended to put 40% of your money into the Gold American Eagle Proof Series and 20% into specialty coins, such as Pre-1933, "W" Mintmarks Eagles and American Buffalo Gold Coins.

Take into consideration the Knight Frank Luxury Index conducted by Knight Frank, a leading independent firm with over 110 years of experience specializing in wealth creation through global property consultancy. The index analyzes the performance of alternative asset categories, including cars, art, wine and coins over time. Published in its 2016 Wealth Report, rare coins saw a 13% price growth over one year. Over five years, rare coins were up 92%, the second best performance after collectible cars. After 10 years, rare coins returned 232%, indicating the strength of long-term holding. Rare coins have also shown to have the lowest price volatility over a 10-year period. These findings suggest that including rare coins within a portfolio could improve overall performance. That's why we recommend putting the majority of your portfolio into high-grade coins.

However, don't forget about silver and platinum. High-performance precious metals, like Silver American Eagle coins and Platinum American Eagle coins, are also essential in diversifying your portfolio for long-term protection and growth. We suggest splitting off 10% of your assets into these two coin categories. After speaking with one of our experienced Account Executives, you may find your personal diversification plan differs slightly from these percentages, but it's imperative to stay diversified and think long-term.

Ownership of precious metals has a long history of safeguarding wealth during periods of economic downturn. However, it's over the past decade in particular that gold, silver and platinum have proven their ability to greatly outperform many other asset types. As economics all over the world continue to struggle with an array of troubling issues, this could point a tremendous upside potential of gold, silver, and platinum. Market predictions even suggest the price of gold could hit new record highs in the future.

From a threatened U.S. dollar to ongoing geopolitical concerns around the world, there are a number of reasons that many people are deciding to move a portion of their assets into government-issued gold in particular. Below are some of the major factors currently influencing the gold market:

THE FEDERAL RESERVE'S RISKY MONETARY POLICY

In a largely misguided attempt to jumpstart the stagnant economy, the Federal Reserve launched numerous asset purchase programs called quantitative easing. From November 2008 until October 2014, the Fed stockpiled billions of dollars' worth of mortgage-backed securities and treasury bonds to the tune of tens of billions of dollars monthly, expanding its balance sheet to more than $4 trillion! This could potentially lower the value of the U.S. dollar, and the long-term ramifications may reach a point from which the economy may never recover.

THE DECLINE OF THE U.S. DOLLAR

Traditionally, the value of gold and the U.S. dollar move in opposite directions. And with research indicating that quantitative easing policies will cause the dollar to lose even more buying power in the years to comes, many are moving money into the safe haven of gold before its price moves any higher. Meanwhile, competition for the dollar strengthens abroad, posing a catastrophic long-term threat to the dollar's status as the world reserve currency.

THE NATIONAL DEBT IS ABOVE
$19 TRILLION AND GROWING

The federal government continues to shirk its responsibilities, suspending the debt ceiling and allowing the national debt to balloon past $19 trillion. That's the equivalent of $60,000 for every man, woman, and child in America. The debt is at a point where it's almost inconceivable that it could be dealt with in an appropriate manner. What will happen to the dollar and the economy without major change?

MUNICIPAL BANKRUPTCIES

In 2013, the city of Detroit filed for Chapter 9 Bankruptcy-the largest municipal bankruptcy in the history of the United States. The city went through a drawn-out legal battle over how the debt should be paid down, and one thing that was not off limits was using city workers' pensions. MSM Money revealed that the cities of New York, Los Angeles, and Chicago could be next in line. If essential city workers can't count on retirement, who can?

CAN BANKS BE TRUSTED?

The country's worst financial downturn since the Great Depression had a number of devastating effects, not the least of which was failure of thousands of U.S. banks. But an even scarier precedent was set overseas when up to 60% of bank deposits were taxed in the nation of Cyprus to pay restitution for the corrupt banking system's failure. This established a terrifying model for "bail-in" plans that put citizens' money at risk.

GEOPOLITICAL ISSUES

During times of turmoil at home and abroad, the price of gold typically increases as people seek the precious metal's safety and stability. With a current laundry list of international issues that includes growing sovereign debt, the possibility of war and the ever-present threat of terror attacks, gold has continued to offer a safe haven in a volatile economy.

GOLD SUPPLY/DEMAND ISSUES

With gold's tremendous performance over the past decade causing record-setting demand around the world, availability of the precious metal has emerged as another of the growing reasons that gold is on the move. Among issues affecting the gold supply are the expense involved with mining it. Gold is limited resource. In fact, gold discoveries have significantly declined. Even in areas were mining continues, no one is quite sure how much gold is left to be removed from the earth.

HEDE AGAINST OTHER ECONOMIC ISSUES

In addition to an imperiled U.S. dollar, issues including out-of-control national debt and ongoing U.S. unemployment are causing people to look for alternative ways to protect their money at a time when citizens can't even trust their banks. This is reason enough to begin diversifying your financial portfolio with legal tender gold, silver, and platinum coins that are fully backed by the government for content, weight, and purity.

THE UNITED STATES MINT

Realizing the need for a national currency, Congress passed the Coinage Act on April 2, 1792. This act authorized the creation of the U.S. mint in Philadelphia, the nation's capital at that time.

Today, the U.S. mint operates production facilities in Denver, Philadelphia, San Francisco and West Point, with nearly all modern U.S. government-issued coins minted at the West Point Military Academy in New York.

The U.S. Mint produces some of the most beautiful gold, silver and platinum bullion coins, as well as numismatic products including proof, uncirculated and commemorative coins.

Throughout our nation's history, gold, silver platinum coins have been great stores of wealth. And to own a U.S. minted coin is to own a piece of American history.

MINTAGE AND POPULATION

The mintage of government-issued gold, silver or platinum coin refers to how many of a specific coin were originally issued by its minting institution. Population refers to the number of a particular coin that has received a certain grade by a coin grading service such as Professional Coin Grading Service (PGCS). Population is particularly important to the potential growth in retail price of a government-issued coin, because it can most determine how rare that coin is and may become.

For example, while a gold proof coin of a certain year may have a total mintage of 10,000 coins produced, the number of coins that grade a perfect PCGS PR-70 may only be several hundred. That would mean that, of the 100,000 coins originally produced, there were fewer than 1,000 coins graded 70 in existence. Low mintage and population generally result in higher numismatic coin pricing.

GRADED COIN CASE BREAKDOWN

The seven areas on the coin case are as follows:

1. Coin's category: EX: "Eagle" which would stand for the Gold American Eagle series.

2. Coin's legal tender domination.

3. Professional Coin Grading Service (PCGS) certified.

4. The coin's type: EX: "PR," which stands for Proof. Its grade: "70" and description: "DCAM" (deep cameo finish).

5. Coin's mint date along with the coin's U.S. Mint production facility. Ex: "W" stands for the U.S. Mint at West Point, New York.

6. The assigned serial number of the coin that protects, guarantees and authenticates the U.S. government gold coin inside the capsule.

7. PCGS holographic verification image.

GRADING

A graded, or certified, gold, silver or platinum coin is one that has undergone careful scrutiny by an independent coin grading service in order to determine the coin's overall condition. Coins are graded on a scale from 1 to 70, with a grade of 70 reserved for coins determined to be flawless.

Grading can be important to the upside potential of a gold, silver or platinum coin, because grade determines the population of a given type of coin, and therefore, its potential rarity. Grading also serves to physically protect a coin because once a grade has been issued, a grading service sonically seals the coin inside an impact-resistant case.

TYPE

PROOF (PR)

Gold proof (PR) coins undergo a special minting process that produces a coin with a beautiful, mirror-like finish. In the case of American Eagles, the proof versions are usually produced in substantially smaller numbers than the mint state (MS) versions.

MINT STATE (MS)

Mint state gold coins, also referred to as "business strikes," are usually produced in much higher numbers than proof coins, and are intended to offer individuals a convenient way to own physical gold. In the case of U.S. Congressional Coins, it's important to state that the mint versions of the coins are typically produced in smaller numbers, which can make them more sought-after due to their rarity.

DATE RUNS AND SETS

Most precious metals coin programs are produced in various denominations. Those programs have all of the denominations for a given year combined into what is known as a set. It is quite an achievement to own a full set for a year of issue, but there is still a far greater accomplishment that rewards a precious metals owner with great profit potential. When a series of consecutive years of sets are acquired, that is called a date run-the ultimate feat.

CERTIFIED COINS VS. BULLION

Bullion is unlike rare and collectible coins that have been examined and graded by a professional grading service. A bullion coin's market value is tied almost entirely to its weight in gold and current market price, making it more liquid, short-term hold. With certified coins, you have the opportunity for greater protection from market fluctuations. Furthermore, diversifying within the certified coin sector allows you to implement a second barrier of security-the numismatic value of the coin. A balance is recommended between the two.

AMERICAN EAGLE GOLD PROOF
U.S. Government-Issued Gold Coin

The spectacular American Eagle Gold Proof Coin enjoys immense popularity due to intrinsic beauty, gold coin content and limited mintages. Produced by the U.S. Mint using a specialized minting process, American Eagle Gold Proofs feature exquisite images that appear to float above the coin's mirror-like surface. These legal tender gold coins are authorized by Congress and backed by the U.S. government for gold content, weight and purity. In all but their first two years of issue (1986-1987), American Gold Proof Coins were minted in four sizes and are commonly purchased as complete sets.

Compared to American Gold Eagle Bullion Coins, American Eagle Gold Proofs are produced in exceedingly limited numbers. This makes them favorites among gold buyers wishing to own coins that may appreciate in price due to their relative rarity. American Eagle Gold Proof Coins feature a stunning Miss Liberty (front) design, originally created by Augustus Saint-Gaudens.

THE SMART WAY TO OWN PROOFS:
COMPLETE SETS AND DATE RUNS

When purchasing American Eagle Gold Proof Coins, it is important to keep in mind that these legal tender coins are minted in only limited numbers from year to year. By law, American Eagle Gold Bullion Coins must be produced in sufficient quantity to meet public demand, while the proof version of the coin is minted for discerning gold buyers and only in quantities the U.S. Mint decides, or is able to produce.

Next, consider that compared with the total number of American Eagle Gold Proof Coins minted each year, a relatively small number typically grade as high as PR-69 or PR-70. Now, imagine owning a 4-coin set ($50, $25, $10, $5) of American Eagle Gold Proofs that all grade that high. Even better, picture a coin portfolio filled with 4-coin PR-69 and Pr-70 American Eagle Gold Proofs Sets from each year the coins were minted (a complete date run). You can begin to see the tremendous potential that entire sets and date runs can possess. The highest-graded full dates run of American Eagle Gold Proof Coins could yield the greatest potential for return in the gold market due to their relatively limited availability.

PROOF MINTING PROCESS

The American Eagle Gold Proof Coin undergoes a fascinating minting process in which burnished gold coin blanks are manually fed into presses that are fitted with highly polished dies. The coins are struck multiple times to achieve the fine details and mirror-like appearance, and inn the end, are painstaking hand checked by white-gloved inspectors at the U.S. mint. This specialized minting process is used to produce only a certain number of American Eagle Gold Proof Coins, and only during years the Mint has sufficient quantities of gold blanks to make them.

HISTORIC DESIGN

The obverse (front) design of the American Eagle Gold Proof Coin is based on one of the true legends of American coinage, the Augustus Saint-Gaudens designed, $20 Double Eagle of 1907-1933. It features the image of Liberty holding a torch and olive branch while rays of the sun shine from behind her. The American Eagle Gold Proof Coin's reverse design was created by sculptor Miley Basiek and features a male eagle carrying an olive branch while flying above a nest containing a female eagle and her hatchlings-true symbols of America.

RONAM NUMERAL DATES

For its first six years (1986-1991), American Eagle Gold Proof Coins were dated using roman numerals. From 1992 through today, American Eagles have used traditional Arabic numbers. Many find the Roman numeral design an element to be significant because, before 2009, the only other U.S. coin to every feature a Roman numeral date was the 1907 High Relief Double Eagle, one of which sold in 2008 for an incredible price of more than $1.4 million.

BULLION

The most widely traded form of gold and silver is bullion. Produced by government mints and private companies, bullion comes in the form of coins, bars and ingots. Coins are the most popular form of bullion due to their portability and fast-liquidity attributes.

You can purchase bullion coins in fractional denominations, which makes precious metals ownership more affordable. Fractional coins also make it easier to diversify your gold and silver portfolio and liquidate portions when desired. Bullion coins are available in one ounce, one-half ounce, one-quarter ounce, and one-tenth ounce denominations.

BULLION VS. PROOF GOLD

The U.S. mint produces the Gold American Eagle mainly in two finishes: mint state (or bullion coins) and proof coins. The proof coins stand apart for two reasons. They have a mirror-like polish, which makes their design appear to float above the background and, more importantly, they have much lower mintage numbers. In high grades, both finishes can present great profit potential, but proof coins are produced in significantly fewer numbers, making them inherently more rare.

"W" MINTMARK AMERICAN EAGLE
U.S. Government-Issued Gold Coin

The "W" Mintmark American Eagle is one of the most unique gold coins the U.S. Mint has produced over the past decade. The extremely popular "W" American Eagle is minted using a specialized process, while also featuring the famous "W" mintmark of the U.S. Mint at West Point, New York.

In addition to a one-ounce gold coin, "W" Mintmark American Eagle Gold coins were all produces in fractional sizes in only 2006, 2007, and 2008. Starting in 2011, the U.S. Mint only produced the "W" in the one-ounce size with extremely low mintages. The 2012 "W" is actually the lowest minted American Eagle currently in the program at just 5,829 produced! It is these limited numbers that could ensure these coins maintain their upside potential.

ULTRA HIGH RELIEF DOUBLE EAGLE
U.S. Government-issued Coin

The 1-ounce, 24 karat 2009 Ultra High Relief Double Eagle was the crowning achievement in the minting of U.S. gold coins. When Theodore Roosevelt called for a "renaissance" in American coinage in the early 1900s, famed sculptor, Augustus Saint-Gaudens, obliged the President by designing a coin that is today considered one of the most beautiful U.S. coins ever minted: the 1907 High Relief Double Eagle Gold Coin.

Though Saint-Gaudens' original designs called for an ultra-high relief coin, minting technology at the time did not allow for a coin of that type to be mass produced. More than 100 years later, the U.S. mint was finally able to realize the 1997 Roosevelt vision and Saint-Gaudens design by creating the 4-mm thick, 2009 Ultra High Relief Double Eagle.

AMERICAN BUFFALO GOLD

U.S. Government-Issued Coin

Authorized by the Presidential $1 Coin Act of 2005, the U.S. Government-Issued American Buffalo Gold Coin was the first .9999 24-karat gold coin ever produced by the U.S. Mint. It features a design based on the classic "Buffalo Nickel" of 1913-1938 and is available in both mint state and proof versions.

Extremely popular since its initial release, the American Buffalo Gold Coin is minted in 24-karat gold, a full 2-karats more than traditional U.S. gold coins (24-karat vs. 22-karat). For the years 2006-2007 and 2009-

2016, the American Buffalo was produced by the U.S. Mint in only 1 oz. size, while in 2008, fractional sizes of 1/10 oz., 1/4 oz., and 1/2 oz. were also minted.

AMERICAN EAGLE PLATINUM PROOF

U.S. Government-Issued Platinum Coin

Since 1997, when the 35th Director of the U.S. Mint Philip N Diehl co-authored the law authorizing its production, the American Eagle Platinum Proof Coin has been one of the most unique and attractive of all modern U.S. legal tender coins. Since platinum is considerably more rare than gold, the U.S. Mint issues these coins in limited numbers, making them that much more attractive.

American Eagle Platinum Proof Coins contain 99.95% pure platinum, and bear the "W" mintmark if the U.S. Mint at West Point. American Eagle Platinum Proof Coins are produced if four U.S. legal tender denominations: 1 oz., 1/2 oz., 1/4 oz. and 1/10 oz. The 1 oz. coin carries a face value of $100, the highest denomination ever to appear on an American coin. From 2009-2015, only the 1 oz. Platinum Proof Coin was produced. The coin's reverse design changes annually.

SILVER CAN HELP SHIELD YOUR WEALTH

In these uncertain times, precious metals, such as silver, can provide a tangible assurance of future wealth.

MORGAN SILVER DOLLAR

Known today simply as the "Morgan Dollar," these coins were designed to give Miss Liberty back her femininity. The observe (front side) depicts her facing left with LIBERTY inscribed on a ribbon holding a spray of leaves and sheaves, while the reverse (back) features a majestic wingspread eagle. Proof coins are available in proportion to the original number of pieces struck.

PEACE SILVER DOLLAR

This curiously-named coin resulted from a competition to find emblems of peace after the First World War. On its reverse, an eagle appears sitting atop the inscription, PEACE, while the observe features Miss Liberty wear a diadem of spikes. Very few Proofs of these coins were made, making them quite valuable as compared to Proofs of other silver dollars on the market.

AMERICAN SILVER EAGLE

The official silver bullion coin of the United States of America features the beloved "Walking Liberty" design (originally minted on the Walking Liberty Half Dollar coin, 1919-1947) on its observe, and a rendition of the Great Seal of the United States of America on its reverse. In addition to the bullion version, a proof version and an uncirculated version kay be available.

SILVER IS THE MOST USEFUL
OF THE PRECIOUS METALS

As far as metals go, silver is the jack-of-all-trades. It has the highest electrical conductivity of any element and the highest thermal conductivity of any metal. This continues to inspire an ever-increasing demand for it in the industrial, electronic, and even textile industries – as it's now being used in medical gowns thanks to its natural anti-bacterial properties.

Today, coins only account for approximately 10% of all silver produced annually. Which means the price of silver is insulated from fluctuations in investment markets that many investors find so disturbing. And with the price of silver currently well below its historical peak, now is an attractive time to buy. Additionally, analysts believe that it will rise with the growth of global economies, market development in emerging and BRIC countries, and expanding worldwide trade.

PRECIOUS METALS ARE ASSETS, NOT MERE INVESTMENTS.

Precious metals, such as silver and gold, have always been a trusted, long-term store of wealth. While they may not make you rich overnight, they will help protect what you've earned.

Unlike paper-based investments that may come and go, precious metals, such as silver, will always have significant value. And since it is a finite resource, only a certain amount will ever be minted into coins -serving as a hedge against inflation risks.

WHAT ARE THE BENEFITS OF OPENING A PRECIOUS METALS IRA?

Hedge your portfolio with a

Precious Metal-backed IRA

In 1986, the IRS began allowing individuals to hold certain precious metals within their individual retirement accounts. Precious Metals IRAs offer a unique hedge against stock market volatility by offering all the tax advantages of traditional, paper-backed IRAs without many of the accompanying uncertainties.

More Distribution Options

When it's time to withdraw from our retirement accounts, a Precious Metals IRA offers an option that traditional IRAs cannot: to take physical possession of your metals and potentially continue to benefit from the growth of your assets. If you so choose, Precious Metal IRAs can also be quickly liquidated.

Tax Deferred Rollover

Rolling over into a gold or silver IRA does not result in any immediate tax obligations. It's simply a lateral transfer from one asset class to another and from one custodian to another.

ADVISORY 9

Hints On Hedging With Property

In inflationary times money moves into what is called hard tangible assets that hold the promise of offering some protection from the ravages of inflation. There are a number of such assets with which you may want to become familiar. Chief among these are gold and silver bullion, rare gold and silver coins, junk silver coins, uncirculated silver dollars, mutual funds that invest in gold stocks, diamonds and colored gemstones, rare stamps, and various investment-grade collectibles.

GOLD

Gold should be looked at as a store of value, not as a medium of speculation. In the past people accumulated gold not because they thought it would bring them value, but because it was a means of representing and preserving the wealth they already had.

The government arbitrarily controlled the price of gold at $35 an ounce for decades while the price for everything else was allowed to rise with inflation. In 1971 the government was literally forced to let the price float freely and it radically went up to regain its price relative to other goods and services. At that time gold became an attractive speculation and went to $200 by 1971. After backing off to $103 in 1976, it climbed to $886 in January of 1980. Once again it backed off and dramatically lost 60 percent of its dollar value.

What does the future hold for gold? I do not know, but you should have some knowledge of this store of value and its place in your portfolio.

Even in normal times gold has held a special attraction. Charles de Gaulle spoke lovingly of "gold, which never changes, can be shaped into ingots, bars, coins, has no nationality, and is eternally and universally accepted as the unalterable fiduciary value." From biblical reference to the gift of the Magi to the gold medals awarded at Olympic competitions, gold has been held in high esteem.

Should gold have a place in your total financial planning? The answer could be yes. Should you use it as your "fail safe" plan in the event other more conventional approaches fail, or regard it as one of the items you should value for its investment merits alone? Should you treat gold as you do fire insurance on your home? If your home doesn't burn down, you probably wouldn't cancel your fire insurance. Or should you treat it as a valuable investment for profit? This you will need to answer for yourself.

Let's say you've determined that a portion of your assets should be in gold or gold-related investments. What approach should you take? Should you invest in gold bullion, gold coins, gold medallions, gold jewelry, gold mining stocks, or mutual funds that invest in gold mining stock?

GOLD DEMAND

There are five types of gold demands: the monetary demand, the industrial commercial demand, the political demand, the inflation-hedging demand, and the depression hedging demand.

Monetary demand. Even though most politicians condemn the backing of gold or silver for paper currency in circulation as archaic, it does have the advantage of limiting the amount of currency and credit governments can create. The supply of money today is growing worldwide at a compound rate of over 10 percent per year, while the gold supply is increasing only around 1-1/2 percent.

I will not go into how the United States has arrived at this point in our history, nor how our country abrogated the Bretton Woods Treaty on August 15, 1971, when we closed the gold window and refused to exchange anymore dollars for gold. Suffice it to say, since that time the world has been pushed onto floating exchange rates that have caused highly unstable fluctuating currencies.

Today, in spite of our often repeated U.S. position that gold is being demonetized, European monetary authorities believe the opposite-that gold is being remonetized. Over 50 percent of the monetary reserves of the world's central banks are held in gold bullion. Arab and Japanese central banks have become particularly active in acquiring gold.

Industrial Demand. In 1981 industrial and jewelry demand for gold absorbed over one-half of the world's production. There were only 1,200 tons of newly mined gold. This demand is growing.

Political Demand. This factor could be the most important. Political demand for gold occurs when there is political turmoil in the world as "smart money" of a particular region moves out of the currency of that region and into the world's most liquid and anonymous instrument, gold. We have seen classic examples in recent years of this "slight capital" exiting Vietnam, Iran, Afghanistan, and Central America moving into gold.

Inflation Hedge. In 1938 you could buy a man's suit for a $20 gold coin or a $20 bill. Today, as we know, that bill would only buy a tie whereas the gold coin would still buy the suit. The gold coin has retained its purchasing power.

When inflation is accelerating, or there is a threat that it will, the demand for gold increases. When the prospects for inflation decrease, the price of gold decreases. The correlation became obvious as the Reagan administration became more and more effective in slowing the inflation rate and the price of gold dipped accordingly.

Gold in Times of Depression.

What has been the record of gold-related investments during times of depression? There are two kinds of monetary turmoil. One is inflation in which money becomes worth less every day, and which causes people to turn to gold to protect their purchasing power. A second kind of monetary turmoil is depression in which money becomes worth more every day. In such circumstances people fear the loss of their money and can also turn to gold, which many consider the ultimate money,

A bit of history may add some perspective. In the early 1930s President Franklin Roosevelt noticed people taking money out of savings and loan associations because of their fears concerning the solvency of these institutions. They put their money into gold. When the savings and loans appeared to be in danger of collapsing, there was no money available from them for mortgages. To help prevent this from happening, President Roosevelt abolished gold ownership in 1933 in order to stimulate the depositing of currency with savings and loan associations. This is precisely what happened after he abolished gold ownership.

(One footnote, perhaps, about the behavior of governments: President Roosevelt abolished gold ownership in 1933 at the official price of $20.67 an ounce, after all of the gold had been turned in, President Roosevelt raised the price of gold to $35.00 an ounce.)

The stock market reached a low in 1932, It took twenty-five years for the Dow Jones Industrial Average to achieve the levels it had reached in 1929. In times of depression people lost confidence in a corporation's ability to produce profit and pay a dividend, or pay interest on bonds that have sold previously. They also lose confidence in a municipality's ability to generate sufficient taxes to not only pay interest on bonds but to retire debt as well.

The result is that in a depression people have turned to gold and to gold mining shares as a mechanism for both income and appreciation.

Ways to Invest in Gold

There are five ways you may invest in gold: mutual funds investing in gold mining shares, gold bullion, gold coins, gold futures, and gold mining ventures.

Mutual Funds Investing in Gold Mining Share.

I personally prefer investing in South African gold mining shares through a well-managed mutual fund for a number of reasons. Usually the prices of the stocks lag behind the bullion itself, giving me an opportunity to see the direction gold prices are moving. Most of the shares outperform the bullion, and they also pay a dividend, which in the past has run as high as 10 percent. There is a daily liquidity by wire or mail. Also, the government could ban the ownership of gold and could require that it be turned in for less than the market value.

South African Political Stability.

Many have expressed a fear of political instability in South Africa, and others have expressed a dislike of some of their racial policies. In regard to their political stability, it is interesting to note that almost every nation except South Africa has replaced its political leaders over the last four to five years either by scandal or a vote of no confidence. Also, the Republic of South Africa has never had a bank failure. The government is also trying to improve the standard of living for everyone in the nation.

Patriotism.

How patriotic is it to invest in South African gold shares? That's a question you may have and should answer yourself. You may believe that if we have monetary turmoil and economic disruption, your patriotic duty is to maintain your purchasing power in real money so that you will have the means of helping rebuild our country in the event an economic disruption should occur. Historically, gold-related investments have been effective in the preservation of capital in times of monetary and economic uncertainty.

Each of us must be a steward of all the assets that we have. To preserve buying power is an obligation of all of us who are socially minded because those who have capital always dictate the ethics and morality of our nation through the type of investments that they make.

Gold Bullion.

(Bars and Wafers). You probably should not consider this way, since it would generally have to be assayed prior to resale. You could consider this method if you are buying a large amount of gold and plan to leave it on deposit at a bank and eventually sell it without ever taking possession.

Gold Coins.

One way you might consider, which is the most popular way, is low-premium coins that trade within a few percent of their bullion content. These coins-such as the 1-ounce Krugerrand, the 1-ounce Canadian Maple Leaf, 1.20-ounce Mexican 50 peso, and the .98-ounce Austrian Corona-are very liquid, require no assay upon resale, and are concentrated forms of wealth in a convenient and anonymous bearer form. These can be purchased at a 3 to 7 percent premium above bullion price.

A large network of gold coin dealers is spread across the United States. They make two-way markets in the popular bullion coins (as well as silver coins and bars). A typical commission is 2-3 percent. You should probably avoid margin coin dealers since leveraged positions in gold coins can be wiped out by sharp short-term fluctuations in these markets. Most gold coins are delivered by the dealer directly to the investor, though larger dealers will store coins for a nominal fee. Most investors keep their coins in a safe-deposit box.

Gold Commodity Futures.

These are highly speculative and very difficult to trade successfully. Go this route only if you are willing to take very speculative risks.

Gold Mining Ventures.

This is covered later.

Investing In Silver.

There was a time when I considered gold to be money and silver a metal. Silver is an industrial metal, but it can offer a hedge against inflation.

In the inflationary surge of the late 1970's, silver rose tenfold from under $5 per ounce to over $50. In the disinflation of 1981 and 1982, it fell back to below $7. If inflation surges again, however, like gold, silver can also be expected to rise.

There are three popular silver investment vehicles in the United States:

1. *Junk Silver Coins*. These are bags of dimes, quarters, and fifty-cent pieces, minted prior to 1965, before the U.S. government replaced the silver in other coinage with plastic and copper. A bag contains $1,000 in face value with a market value of $6,300 in mid-1982.

2. *Silver Bars*. These bars come in sizes pf 1, 10, and 1,000-ounce, the 100-ounce bar being by far the most popular. Only bars from well-known refiners, such as Englehard, Johnson Mathy, or Credit Suisse, should be purchased. These well-known bars will not have to be assayed upon repurchase.

3. *Uncirculated Silver Dollars*. These dollars, minted in the late 1800s and early 1900s, were for the most part melted down over the years. The few that remained were held either collectors or the Federal Reserve Banks until the 1950s and 1960s. Morgan or Peace Silver Dollars have had very favorable price appreciation in recent years because of both their silver content and their scarcity (or numismatic value). They tend to be much less volatile in price than gold or silver.

Rare Coins

Rare (numismatic) U.S. coins can be another way to preserve capital. They date back to 1793, were coined in gold and silver, and are in low supply owing to the small number originally produced and the subsequent melting that has occurred.

They are a highly concentrated, portable store of wealth and are not subject to governmental regulation or exchange controls; and in the past they have been excluded when government confiscation of gold and silver have occurred.

Over 75 percent of U.S. rare coins are held by long-term investors, a factor that should give underlying price stability.

Numismatic coins are not as liquid as bullion coins but there are over 3,500 U.S. coin dealers.

What makes a Coin Valuable?

You may ask, What makes a coin valuable? It is more than age, condition, date, type, or metal content. A great deal depends on its rarity and its supply and demand. There are approximately fifteen grades of excellence recognized by the American Numismatic Association, ranging from *Proof*, the mirror-like finish of a coin that was manufactured by the Mint and then carefully preserved from any nocks and scratches, all the way to fifteenth grade, *Good*, which actually means "Very heavily worn with portions of lettering, date, and legends worn smooth. The date may be barely readable."

Prices of rare coins have been rising steadily, year after year. It appears that this trend will continue, for there is a static supply of coins-and there will never be very many more available than there are now-while there is an increasing demand as more and more collectors crowd into the field. As you've learned by now, when demand is greater than supply, prices tend to rise.

Here are some of the features and potential benefits that well-selected numismatic coins can offer:

Feature	Possible Benefit
Potential appreciation	Growth, assets increase
Diversification	Risk spreading can lower losses, allow appreciation in other areas.
Inexpensive entry	Small amount of money needed to initially establish an account.
Anonymity	Maximum protection and discretion.
Long-term capital gain	Gains on coins held one year qualify for long-term capital gains treatment.
Tax-free exchange	When coins are exchanged rather than sold, tax payment is deferred until finally sold for cash.
Durability	No special handling or environmental considerations necessary. Careless handling can be avoided by special coin handlers.

Insurable	If lost or stolen, the entire investment is not lost
Easy maintenance	Cost to maintain is no more than a safety deposit box.
Relatively high liquidity	Coins may be tendered to a coin dealer at wholesale, or consigned to a commissioned auctioneer.

Rare Coins Limited Partnership

At this point in our discussion you may have been impressed with the investment potential of rare coins, but do not have the interest or perhaps the time to develop expertise in them. If this is where you find yourself, you may want to consider Rare Coin Limited Partnerships. Each unit is $500 and the minimum purchase is five units, or a minimum investment of $2,500.

Rare Stamps

Another area you may want to familiarize yourself with is rare stamp collecting. It is one of the most popular hobbies in our nation, with over twenty million collectors here and fifty million around the world. Most people who collect rare stamps consider it a hobby, but there are growing numbers of persons who are buying stamps as an investment and are finding it very profitable.

Stamp investing, highest quality of course, has yielded about a 12 percent per year rate of return on investment for the past two decades. Philately, as stamp collecting is referred to in trade circles, is a fairly big business. Around a billion dollars in sales occur each year, and it is estimated there are in excess of fifty million collectors worldwide. There appears to be no scarcity of willing investors, but dealers are beginning to complain that they cannot obtain enough quality stamps to sell-again a situation where demand exceeds supply.

The top-priced stamp at resent is the British Guyana Magenta one cent, appraised at $9,480,000.

Some rules you may want to follow when investing in rare stamps are:

1. Begin as a collector, and work into becoming an investor.

2. Diversify in stamps.

3. Choose only top-quality stamps.

4. Look for stamps that are old, clean, undamaged, and of course, rare. If you do not have the inclination or time to do this on your own, work with a financial planner who is knowledgeable in this area.

Why have rare stamps performed so well? Some characteristics that they possess that may be of interest to you are:

1. *Price Appreciation.* Stamps have outdistanced the rate of inflation. Their prices are maintained because of the unflagging interest of fifty million collectors throughout the world.

2. *Safety.* Prices tend to rise in both good times and bad times. Stamps are portable and can be used as a shield against political or economic unrest.

3. *Tax Advantage.* An investment in stamps is taxed only when you sell them and then at the lower capital gains rates. You are also allowed to take deductions for any expenses incurred in connection with your investment, such as a safe-deposit box, insurance, and so on.

4. *High Liquidity.* There is a steady, active market for quality stamps. New collectors and investors are constantly entering the market. It may actually be easier to sell rare stamps than to buy them.

5. *Ease of Maintenance.* Stamps can be easily protected, transported, and insured. When stamps are kept in a safe-deposit box. Insurance rates are extremely low.

The Economics of Diamonds

"Diamonds are forever." "Diamonds are a girl's best friend." These are the ads most familiar to us. Are they forever the best investment? The answer is no, not every year, but over the long run the prices of high-quality investment-grade diamonds have kept ahead of inflation.

The brilliance and durability of diamonds have always humans, and the desire for them has not diminished over the years. However, in the last few decades the beauty of diamonds became secondary, and they began to be viewed more and more in terms of their investment potential. Those who live in the United State have been slow in catching up to the awareness of this

174

potential, but Europeans and Third world businessmen have recognized it for years.

In typical fashion, once alerted to the possibilities, U.S. investors jumped into the market with enthusiasm and vigor, often without significant information or the background to make wise decisions.

Since investment-grade diamonds can be considered viable part of a diversified portfolio, you should become more knowledgeable about this area of investing. The information I'll present here will not be sufficient to make you an expert on the subject, but it should make you more knowledgeable, teach you a few do's and don'ts, and whet your appetite for further information.

Diamonds have long been a haven for some of the assets of the very rich. Worldwide affluence is a relatively recent phenomenon. Europeans have a much longer tradition of mistrust of governments and fiat currencies than do we Americans. Consequently, gemstone investing has a much older history in Europe. This demand has accelerated during the past few years, raising the prices and pulling the better quality stones to markets outside our country.

Beauty, Durability, Rarity

All gems have three attributes in common. They are beautiful; they are durable; and they are rare. Beauty may be in color, iridescence (as in pearls or opals), or fire (as in diamond). Durability is necessary for a valuable gem-pearls are soft, yet durable. A diamond is the only colorless, transparent gemstone that has all three of these qualities. It stands alone in its ranking of gemstones for its transparent, colorless beauty, as well as its rarity and durability.

Since the nineteenth century, the major mining center for diamonds has shifted from India to South Africa. South Africa experienced a "Diamond Rush" in the 1860s very much like California's Gold Rush. The rarity of diamonds is underlined by the fact that fewer and fewer of the finest gemstones are being found.

Costly to Mine

Searching for the diamond of high value is not unlike looking for the proverbial needle in the haystack. It is estimated that current procedures may require mining from 45 to 200 tons of rock or sand to uncover one carat (2/10 of one gram or 1/142 of an ounce) of quality diamond, an extremely costly and arduous process. Approximately 80 percent of all diamonds are found unsuitable for jewelry or investment and are used for industrial purposes. The industrial diamond, because of its color, structural defects, size, or shape, does not meet the high standards required for gemstones. Of the remaining 20 percent, only about 3 percent are considered to be of investment grade. And of this 3 percent, only 1 percent will yield a gemstone of at least one carat in size.

Today diamonds are mined not only in South Africa, but also in South-West Africa (Namibia), Angola, Australia, Russia (20 percent of the world's supply), Brazil, and India. U.S. production so far has ben quite modest.

Monopolistic Control

The major control for distribution of diamonds is by the DeBeers Consolidated Mines of South Africa, Ltd. Since the 1930s, DeBeers has held an ironclad monopoly on the diamond industry that amounts to from 60 to 85 percent of the world's supply. The Central Selling Organization (CSO), the wholesaler arm of DeBeers, purchases rough diamonds not only from the DeBeers mines (18 percent of the world's supply), but also from other producers. The distribution of the diamonds is controlled through "sights" or sales that are held ten times each year by the DeBeers. At these sights, packages are made up of the rough high-grade stones, as nearly as possible according to the requirements that have been previously stated to DeBeers, which insures a firm control on the price. DeBeers' stated policy is "to maintain a high degree of price stability for gems and diamonds at all times". While this method of control has been questioned, it has not been broken. Major producers and cutters cooperate with Debeers because they agree that control and stability are good for the industry as well as for DeBeers.

The select group of 230 buyers invited to the "sights" may refuse to purchase a packet, but they rarely do, as hundreds of other buyers could easily replace each one. After the purchase of the parcels from DeBeers, the buyers, if they are dealers, sort the packages into categories for their own customers. If they are cutters, they will divide the rough package into the group they plan to sell, and the stones that will be cut under their supervision. Each stone must be evaluated, and the master cutter must use his skill and professional judgement in deciding the most practical shape and size for that particular stone before the work is begun. Then cutting, shaping facets, and polishing will all be a part of the process.

The Four Cs

Cut. The "cut" of a diamond refers to its proportions and dimensions, based on certain measurements. The brilliance of the diamond depends not only on the light reflected from the surface, but on the rays that have been partly absorbed before being refracted. The diamond is exceptionally reflective: about 17 percent of the light falling directly on its surface will be reflected back, accounting for its "life" (compared with about 5 percent of light falling on a transparent glass stone). Diamond will also absorb 80 percent of the light entering before it is refracted, creating the diamond's "fire". The perfectly cut diamond maximizes the amount of light returned to the viewer; hence, the more finely proportioned the stone, the higher the value.

The word "cut" is also used to mean the "shape" of the stone, or the design of its finished form. While unusual shapes may be used, many cutters choose one of the five most popular shapes or cuts:

1. The familiar Round-Brilliant with fifty-eight facets has been a favorite in rings and other types of jewelry for centuries. In tiny sizes, with only eighteen facets, it may be used as a side stone in the setting when it is called a single cut. Eighty percent of all polished diamonds are Round-Brilliants.

Three modern variations of the Brilliant cut are also among the most often selected:

2. The Marquise-Brilliant is usually long and narrow, in a pointed boat shape. In the setting of a ring, this shape tends to make the fingers look slim. Because of the additional labor required for the cutting, it may be

more expensive than a Round-Brilliant stone of the same size and quality. Also, the Marquise may be chosen by the cutter to maximize the unflawed portion of a stone.

3. The Pear-shaped Brilliant is another popular cut for jewelry. The world's largest fashioned diamond, the Cullinan I, or the Great Star of Africa, is pear-shaped. The original size of the rough diamond was 3,106 carats.

4. The Oval-Brilliant is also an adaptation of the Round-Brilliant. It may appear to be even larger than a Round-Brilliant of the same carat weight.

5. The Emerald cut, so called because emeralds are often cut this way, is rectangular or square. Its facets are polished diagonally across the corners.

After the diamond has been cut and polished, the finished product will be sold to importers, wholesalers, or distributors. There are about ten exclusive cash, markets, or Bourses, in the world, one of which is the Diamonds Dealers Club in New York. The diamond trade is extremely secretive and security conscious. Once a grudgingly bestowed membership is gained for the clubs, business is conducted on the principles of trust and credit. The loss of that trust by simply refusing to purchase a stone once accepted can ruin the perpetrator forever in diamond circles.

Purchasers select stones from the cutter with the greatest care. Other features in addition to the cut and proportion that increase the value of a gem are the color, clarity, and carat weight.

Color. Diamonds come in a full range of colors, including red, pink, blue, and yellow, with the highest grade of color for a diamond being the whitest possible, or colorless. As color is detected in a stone, its value decreases as the hue deepens. This is true until the diamond reaches the optimum point-when the shade is so rich that the value rises precipitously. This rare and quite valuable color is termed a "Fancy." Fancy diamonds are in great demand for investment stones as well as for jewelry.

Techniques and systems for color grading of polished diamonds may vary to a significant extent among diamond exchanges and dealers throughout the world, but the determination is becoming increasingly scientific because of the spectrophotometer. This instrument measures the nitrogen content of the stone; more nitrogen means a deeper color. The spectrophotometer is an instrument commonly used in research by industry for measuring absorption and directional reflectance. Specially modified for diamond-color grading, it is used to measure specific wave lengths of reflectance, comparing the diamond to pure barium sulphate powder as a standard of whiteness.

Clarity. The third C is clarity. The clarity of a stone is another factor that governs its price. Clarity is defined as the degree of internal perfection, or the degree to which the stone possesses inclusions, or irregularities, which may diffuse or scatter light. Undesirable reflections may be caused by the presence of foreign matter within the stone, surface defects, minute cracks, natural strains in the crystals, or certain other imperfections. The method of quantifying clarity is a point system generally based on the size of the inclusion, its position, and the extent to which it interrupts the optimum passage of light. The terminology established by the Gemological Institute of America is generally used: it runs from FLAWLESS to VERY VERY SLIGHT INCLUSIONS, to VERY SLIGHT INCLUSIONS, to IMPERFECT. For a diamond to be regarded as FLAWLESS, it must free of external blemishes as well as being clean internally. While FLAWLESS is the top grade for clarity, it is something of a misnomer, for rarely if ever is a stone completely flawless. This grade may possess some modest irregularities that cannot be considered to materially affect the brilliance of the diamond.

Carat. The fourth factor affecting value is the carat weight. This is a familiar standard, but must not be confused with the "karat" used to describe the fineness of gold. The origin of the carat measurements was the seed from the carob tree. This tiny seed was so uniform in weight and shape that Middle Eastern gem traders used it as a gauge in weighing diamonds. The international standard of the carat weight is .2 grams, while each carat is divided into 100 points. For example, a ¾ carat stone would weigh exactly 75 points, or 75 percent of the weight of one carat, or .15 grams. In determining carat weight, laboratories use extremely accurate caratronal electronic scales that weigh to one-thousandth part of a carat. This sophisticated equipment is believed essential to proper evaluation, since carat size is a prime factor in assessing the value of the diamond.

Cost

The passage of a stone from the cutter to wholesaler to jewelry manufacturer to jewelry wholesaler to retailer creates a chain of markups that escalates the price of the ordinary buyer. Thus the value of a diamond as an investment is best realized when dealing at the cutter's level. Also, the price spread is not linear or predictable by carat weight. A small stone may have a 200-300 percent spread, whereas a large stone of two or more carats may have no more than a 20percent spread.

Liquidity

Suppose you need to turn your stones into cash. Liquidity of diamonds falls somewhere between that of gold coins and real estate. They are more liquid than real estate but less liquid than gold coins. Diamonds are a relatively long-term investment and should not be purchased with a speculator's eye for quick, overnight profit. On the other hand, diamonds do represent a tremendous opportunity for concentrated wealth that occupies a minimum amount of space and causes a minimum amount of nervousness wen reading the financial page of the newspaper each morning.

Inflation Hedge

Have investment-grade diamonds properly bought offered a hedge against inflation? The answer is yes, over the long term, but in the early 1980s they became overpriced and declined in price, even though the long-term outlook seems to be upward. DeBeers sets the price of diamonds against the world's strongest currency, with an eye on the inflation charts. Since the United States accounts for approximately 55 percent of the world's market for diamonds, the rate of inflation in the United States has been a large factor in the pricing. Worldwide inflation, or course, must also be considered. For example, the rate of inflation of countries with major cutting centers, such as Israel, must be taken into account.

Stable Stores of Value

Fundamental to the long-term dependability of the diamond market has been the power of DeBeers. As stated above, the cartel has controlled up to 85 percent of the world's diamond supply through controlled distribution. The percentage is not fixed, however, and has been known to slip as low as 60 percent. The continued maintenance of stability is based on the belief by the world's suppliers that the cartel serves the best interest of the industry as a whole.

It is difficult to argue with the success of the past, but it is also impossible to predict who will attempt to break the monopoly in the future. The huge outreach of DeBeers makes it unlikely that its grasp will be loosened in the near future, but challengers will be seeking ways to sell independently. One likely development in the next decade will be more companies attempting a vertical control on their own. In trying to crack the market, they could easily flood it with supplies that would send prices tumbling. Once again, it must be emphasized that any investment has its risk. To succeed, DeBeers must continue to balance the needs of producers against those of major cutters, as well as to convince both groups that continued control is in their best interest as well as possible. On balance, the danger of undercutting the cartel is not sufficiently dire to warrant withdrawal from diamond investing. DeBeers has not gained its position without learning how to maintain that status.

The plan of the company is to extend its influence further into the areas of cutting and marketing. Nevertheless, there will continue to be both smuggling operations and small governments' determined efforts to market diamonds independently. DeBeers expects this. You should also.

The wild card in this scenario is the Russians. Up until now, Russians have worked primarily through the cartel. The fine reputation of the Russian polished diamonds, however, creates the possibility of an independent marketing effort on their part or a price war generated by their unilateral offering of rough stones. The Russia intent in marketing diamonds is unpredictable, but it would seem that stability would be in their best interest, since diamonds constitute a major export for them to buy the foodstuffs the have not be able to produce.

The politics of any of the producing countries could potentially affect the diamond market. Past unrest in South Africa created some apprehension on the part of the distributors. It should be remembered in this regard that the DeBeers Central Selling Organization has had extensive experience negotiating with many different regimes. A shift in government would not alter the need for marketing, while temporary disruption of the producing mines could only enhance the value of investment diamonds.

Scarcity

A much more crucial future certainly is the eventual depletion of the world's natural diamond supply. While too much may be made of this, since there is obviously a limit to "the world's supply" of any natural resource, the fact remains that diamond supplies are dwindling.

How to Invest

After learning what you have thus far about diamonds, if you feel they are worthy of some of your investment dollars, there are certain criteria to follow and pitfalls to avoid.

First, deal only with reputable persons or firms. This is the first, primary, and essential criterion for choosing wisely. Unfortunately, the recent upsurge of interest in diamonds has brought the usual pack of charlatans who capitalize on consumer fads and naiveté. The publicized stories of zirconium switches and telephone sales tend to make buyers uneasy. But reputable firms do exist. Care should be taken to get recommendations and to investigate past records. A gemstone should not be bought from a person or firm without strong backing. Also, as a general rule, one should not buy an investment stone from a jeweler. The jeweler is at the end of the escalating price chain within the industry and seldom can give the best prices. In addition, most jewelers do not have access to the quality of stone that would be considered investment grade.

Second, the selection of a stone must be made with care. This does not mean merely looking at the beauty of gems displayed on black velvet. It means, rather, the selection of a stone that maximizes the qualities described above (color, clarity, cut, carat weight, and proportion) in line with the amount of money you have to invest. The best investment is still the Round-Brilliant cut, H or better color, with at least ½ and hopefully one carat or more in size. Once the parameters of the possible choice have been defined, it will be our pleasure to see a selection of stones within these guidelines and appreciate the beauty of the diamond chosen. This, however, is not completely necessary. More important is the transaction with the trusted broker, mentioned above, and the most important aspect, the certification of the stone by an independent laboratory such as the Gemological Institute of America.

Certification

If you have taken the first precaution (in choice of broker0, certification will be an automatic procedure, with the cost probably absorbed by the company. You should be very careful in dealing with any sellers who claim to do their own certification. In addition to the independent certification, many companies offer a period of thirty days or more in which a stone may be returned without question. Within that period, if there is reason to want it, you may get a second certification of the stone, which, of course, should duplicate the first description if both are done properly. A possible trend in diamond security is the use if sealed packages for gems, once certified. While this may seem an ideal solution to the potential of switching stones, it really does not eliminate the possibility, since the seal must be broken in any case if verification is absolute, and packets may be switched as easily as stones.

Certification of a polished diamond is one of the most important developments in the industry. It is of special significance for investment goods, since each diamond has its own "fingerprints" which make it unique. The importance of securing independent certification cannot be overemphasized.

Third, you should plan carefully with your financial planner the percentage of your total assets that should be hard assets.

Fourth, think of diamonds as a long-term investment, not a short speculative venture. Two years should be the minimum time for you to consider holding a stone; much longer is better.

Fifth, in case it should be necessary to liquidate your investment in the future, check beforehand how to resell. Many companies make a resale-on-consignment service available to their diamond customers, although they will not guarantee a repurchase because of the risk of having the sale classified as a security by the SEC. Also, diamond marketing is carried on in the United States through computer listings, brokers, and companies that sell investment stones. Just as you should not purchase your investment diamonds from the typical jeweler, neither should you sell them through that avenue.

Sixth, plan to protect your investment through careful maintenance. Diamonds are the easiest of all hard assets to store and care for. Vaults or safe-deposit boxes are available, and adequate insurance is easy to obtain. Of course, careful records and safekeeping of the certificates are vital. Though it's probably best not to do so, if you choose you can have your diamonds mounted and enjoyed as jewelry. Even though we recommend storage in a safe-deposit box, I daresay the majority of owners will be wearing them.

Colored Gemstones

The advisability of investing in investment-quality colored gemstones is also worthy of your study. These stones are from twenty to forty times rarer than diamonds and are available for from 17 to 50 percent of the price per carat. Some guidelines you should consider are:

1. *Purchase top quality.* Every gemstone occurs in a range of quality. For example, a ruby can be opaque, filled with cracks and inclusions, or can be a relatively undesirable color. As such it can sell for as little as $5-10 per carat. However, the very finest ruby has sold in recent months for as much as $100,000 per carat. Between these extremes there is a very wide range of quality, involving color, clarity, cutting quality, and size. Investment grade, therefore, can be simply defined as that quality grade for a given type of gemstone for which the supply does not meet demand, so that the result is an increase in price. In general, the higher quality grade, the faster the rise in value in a given period of time. The relationship is not necessarily linear. Historically, the rate of increase in value of the very finest gems has been very much greater than the rise in value of stones just a few grades lower in quality.

2. *Keep up to date on the market.* All gemstones do not increase in value at the same rate. Some types of gems are better known than others and the marketplace and their track record for appreciation are better developed. For example, the supplies of rubies are being depleted at a faster rate than those of emeralds causing the supply-demand equation to yield higher prices and a faster rate of growth for rubies.

3. *Deal with a reputable investment company.* Some types of commodities, such as gold and silver bullion coins (for example, Krugerrands), corporate stocks, bonds, and the like are interchangeable. One Krugerrand is almost identical to any other in terms of appearance, weight, and gold content. Therefore, a verbal description of the commodity is sufficient in its marketing. In the case of most collectables, however, a

standard language that is universally accepted for describing such objects does not exist.

4. *Open market.* Purchase investment gems from firms that operate in an open-market system. A major source of liquidity in the gemstone market is the existence of public auctions. Some major auction houses specialize in the sale of fine gemstones and jewelry; items sold in this manner are listed, and sometimes pictured, in widely disseminated catalogs. The auction house gets a commission from both the buyer and seller, but the sale price of the item is determined by the bidders.

The resale of a gemstone is not much different from the sale of any collectable or tangible commodity. In general, such sales are best carried out through brokers.

5. *Certification.* AGL, IGI, and United States Gemological Services.

6. *Cyclical.* Be prepared to hold your stones because appreciation can be cyclical.

If you are considering colored gemstones as an investment possibility, I recommend that you become very familiar with them before making any purchases. The gemstones you will want to become familiar with-and probably in this order-are: ruby, sapphire, emerald, topaz, peridot, tourmaline, spinel, aquamarine, tanzanite, tsvaorite, garnet, zircon, and chrysoberyl.

Gemstones have been considered a form of money since the beginning of civilization. Their value is known in all societies. Interest in this form of tangible wealth tends to increase in periods of inflation and global influence, as is reflected in their increased demand.

No individual or group has control over the supply of any colored gemstone. The marketplace is structured, yet exceedingly diffuse. The chain of supply is, in most cases, extremely long. Markups tend to be high all along the chain. No government regulates the supply or price of gemstones-the marketplace is one of the last vestiges of free enterprise.

Do be a knowledgeable entrepreneur if you decide to journey forth.

Collectibles

What are collectibles and should you invest in them? It is recommended that you approach your collecting as something to be enjoyed. You'll probably do a better job of learning about the subject, and even if you don't make money you will have had some fun.

Collectibles include a broad range of tangible goods that usually have in common some degree of: (1) rarity, (2) scarcity, (3) demand, (4) popularity, (5) craftsmanship, (6) antiquity or age, (7) aesthetic qualities of beauty and taste, (8) absolute or classical value to our society and culture. Collectibles include the serious investments such as rare coins, rare stamps, rare books, antiques (furniture, dolls, and classic antique cars), art (oil paintings, prints and sculpture), and oriental rugs and carpets. On the other hand, collectibles also include the more faddish, perhaps less prudent, and yet irresistible nostalgia items-toys, Mickey Mouse watches, beer cans, gum machines, movie magazines, table radios, old opera records, baseball cards, old cameras and "photographia" parts and photos, stock certificates, tea and tobacco tins,

Coke signs, Coke trays, penny arcade machines, coin-operated flip-card peep shows, Beatles albums, memorabilia of singers of the 1950s, old Life magazines, "Peanuts" memorabilia, patriotic items, cast iron and tin toys, zeppelin toys, old radio giveaways (Tom Mix, Jack Armstrong, The Lone Ranger, and the like), movie posters, memorabilia of the moon landing and the list goes on and on.

Investing vs. Collecting

Of course, collecting for investment purposes is an entirely different game from collecting collectibles merely for the sake of collecting. The latter practice is considered more of an exhilarating hobby, a treasure hunt, and a means to exhibit a display case of proud possessions. Investing in collectibles can be a method by which money is made and can be calculated and serious business. In fact, investing in collectibles has become so common that some large brokerage houses have established a full gamut of services for the collector-investor who wishes to enter the collectibles marketplace. Experts are available to advise their clients on how to make a prudent investment in a collectible specialty area, how to diversify, and how to make profits in collectibles both in the short term and over the long term.

A number of trust companies that manage the finances of many wealthy individuals now recommend that their clients put some of their funds into art, antiquities, and other tangible holdings in order to protect their funds from inflation and taxes.

A partner of an old and highly respected brokerage firm recently said, "Obviously, investors are more impressed with the return on things that continue to outperform traditional investments." In their last study on comparative yields of tangibles, they reported tat Chinese ceramics headed the list with a ten-year compound rate of return of 19.2 percent per year. Next in line were high-grade American stamps, producing 15.4 percent per year; them paintings by old masters, yielding 13 percent per year; as well as nongold U.S. coins, producing 13 percent per year, all for a period of ten years.

The Fascination with Tangible assets

This increasing interest in investing in collectibles and tangibles can be attributed to several factors: affluence, nostalgia, inflation fears, confiscatory taxes, increased leisure time, disenchantment with other forms of investment, and well-publicized accounts of "soaring" prices of collectibles. Much of the fascination with collectibles appears to be as related to stiff taxes as it is to inflation, for profits in them often elude the tax collector, unlike the gains on securities. The collectible marketplace operates in a free-market atmosphere. There is little or no regulation. There is a free wheeling-dealing atmosphere where markets are cornered to make a sale at a profit and where there is no Sec to interfere.

You will find that dealers in collectibles are similar to stockbrokers, except their credentials are not regulated in the conventional stock brokerage ways. You will find a significant number of excellent dealers, both small and large, who are totally honest. However, you must be cautious, for any area as unregulated as this one will also attract the opposite type of dealer-one who is dishonest, one who may even receive your payment without delivering your purchase to you, or who may sell forgeries and counterfeits as if they were the "real things."

American Quilts-An Example

In the White House, behind Vice President Walter Mondale's desk was an American antique quilt made by one of the Amish people.

Collecting these quilts and using them for wall hangings has become quite popular. If they hold some appeal to you, you may want to consider them as a collectible. Prices begin around $1,000. Most of them are in the somber colors of black, purple, and dark blue and have geometric designs that look striking in modern interiors. The fine stitching and the sophisticated color schemes are their outstanding features. Incidentally, you will find a deliberate mistake in each of them to illustrate that only God is perfect.

A combination of striking design, color harmony, and the fine needlecraft are the characteristics most sought after.

Disadvantages vs. Advantages of Investing in Collectibles

Besides the apparent disadvantages of some "wheeler dealers" in the marketplace, there are other disadvantages and pitfalls you'll want to know about before making a commitment of any kind to this type of investing. Because the positives tend to outweigh the negatives, I'll present the disadvantages first:

1. There is no spot price for collectibles-a collectible has a spread between the bid price and ask prices which can run as much as 30 percent per item.

2. There is a sales tax on a collectible item added to its price when you keep it in the state in which you purchased it, and this can turn out to be a sizable amount.

3. The extra money spent on the spread and the sales tax means that the collectible must be bought with the idea for holding it for at least eighteen months to two years, and selling it then only if the market is right.

4. Not all collectibles have kept pace with inflation. Generally speaking, high-grade coins and art and antiques, when professionally selected, have done as well as the very best kinds of investments available, and continue to do so.

5. Prices of collectibles can "skid".

6. The collectible market is fraught with fakes and flawed merchandise. When a collectible starts coming into demand, the forgers may grind out reproductions in massive quantities.

7. Many hundreds of "get-rich-quick" and other spurious investment schemes have occurred in the collectibles market. All are risky, some are rip-offs.

8. collectibles do not pay interest or dividends. They often entail such costs as insurance and storage. They may be difficult to sell within the timetable you have set.

9. Their profits may be a bit deceptive. For instance, the collector-investor may have bought a Victorian clock for $1,000 and sold it at an auction five years later for $1,500. On first blush, that may seem good. But after paying the auction $300, he only has

1,200 left; so his net gain is only $200, or 4 percent a year. So he didn't win the money game.

The Advantages

None of these disadvantages should necessarily discourage you from becoming better informed about collectibles. They can pay off, both in enjoyment as well as in financial rewards.

1. Collectibles have outperformed many more conventional types of investments.

2. With the lifting of exchange controls in Britain, which enables British individual investors and pension funds to invest abroad, there should continue to be a large number of potential buyers of American collectibles and antiquities. This should help support prices.

3. The willingness on the part of financial planners, banks, investment firms, brokerage houses, and auction houses to inform and advise their clients makes expert advice much more available to you and to others interested in collectibles as investments.

4. The proliferation of investment syndicates formed by doctors, lawyers, and other professional groups in our country has made it possible for quality items to be bought by many more persons than just the wealthiest tycoons in America.

5. The spectacular mega-exhibits on tour in the United States, such as King Tut, have promoted and publicized antiquities and rarities, and are probably accountable for much of the new popularity in rarified Egyptian art treasures. Other exhibits have had similar good effects on art investments.

6. When you sell your collectibles, your profits, if you have held them for a year, will be taxed at the more favorable capital gains rate. Another tax advantage that may fit your planning needs and philanthropic nature is to give your collectibles to a museum or a university. This will enable you to take deductions of as much as 30 percent of your adjusted gross income for up to five years.

7. Because the tangibles' trading market has not been tapped yet by federal regulation, you have greater freedom. This in itself can be very advantageous by affecting their investment potential.

Guidelines on Investing in Collectibles

1. Purchase only what you wish to specialize in; if it is something you like, all the better, as it will maintain your high level of interest over the next ten years and decades thereafter.

2. Buy the best you can afford, even if you must accept limited quantities at first. If possible, purchase your collectibles from a dealer who will guarantee your purchase price back in the future if you trade in for a higher quality.

3. Confine your purchases to collectibles in excellent condition. These will always enjoy outstanding resale value. Look for quality-to be a fine buy, it should be in mint condition. Find out its rarity and its value, as well as its most recent price; verify its date; and determine how many of such items were made.

4. A collectible of any real value should carry a ticker guaranteeing its origin and, in case of very fine items, its travels as well.

5. The authenticity of the collectible should be guaranteed against a full cash refund.

6. Read as much literature as you can on the subject.

7. Attend auctions, wander through antique stores, talk to people, and familiarize yourself completely with the area of interest before you buy anything. Study your line of collectibles for quality, art form, and all aspects of its category.

8. Buy only from reputable dealers or reputable auctions.

9. Become attuned to holding your collectibles for long periods of time. You must allow time for the markup to cover the difference between wholesale and retail prices.

10. If you are a novice, purchase and specialize in collectibles of known and proven work with a history of regular price appreciation.

11. Be aware of antique shops with large selections and fancy frames. Theses angles can lead to overvaluation of the piece itself.

12. Undergo a "comparison-shopping" spree before you actually purchase your item. If you are considering a major purchase, call in a professional appraiser.

13. Be informed and up to date on all prevailing economic and political trends that will influence the collectibles market. A rising stock market can result in extra discretionary income for investors and therefore, a likelihood of surplus funds for items such as antiques. The reverse can have the opposite effect.

14. At auctions, try to spot the dealers in the crowd. Generally, they bid inconspicuously, but the auctioneer

usually knows them. Look for "quick glances" between the auctioneer and his know customer. It may pay to outbid the dealers. They are planning to pay wholesale prices.

15. Regarding sealed bids, bid what you are ready to pay, and don't expect to get the item to a lower price.

16. When bidding from the floor, start high. Continued bidding from a low level stirs up crowd interest. On the other hand, a high bid can knock competition out of the game before the crowd knows what is happening.

17. Don't be afraid to go to the top for advice, even if you are a small investor. Such establishments as Sotheby's and Christie's of New York have been known for their extreme courtesy to all clients, big and small.

18. Always arrange and investigate trucking arrangements, insurance, storage areas such as bank vaults or safe-deposit boxes, storage fees, pick-up terms, burglar alarms, and other security precautions, before buying the actual items.

19. When choosing the collectible you wish to invest in, apply the old truism, "Follow the smart money." This means that one way to find a shrewd investment is to observe the actions of the wealthy, the sophisticated, and those who have demonstrated beyond question their acquisitive abilities.

Collecting Quality Art

Another area that merits your study and research is collecting art. In this area there tends to be agreement among the experts that those who collect art primarily for profit frequently lose, but that those who collect what they love usually make a substantial profit. You will find that collecting art-paintings, drawings, prints and sculpture-can be a delightful, affordable, and profitable investment. Paintings used to be the classic rich man's collectible, that is, the Mellons, the Fricks, and Guggenheims. Now we Americans are behaving much like these millionaires and much like the Europeans-seeking both pleasure and profit in the investment of art.

The necessary components of a good art investment are: rarity, condition, and historical importance. Taste, which is of course subjective, should also be considered. A beautiful picture by a good artist will usually bring more money over a period of years than a great picture that is ugly by a more important artist.

You will probably find as you study this medium that a good art collector is one who buys with both eyes and heart. Underlying every collection that turns out to be a lucrative investment is almost always an undeniable urge to enjoy art.

Quality art has not ridden the crest of the tangible wave, but it has been a tide unto itself. Fine art, though it doesn't have the liquidity of a stock, can be sold in the New York city art world in not more than a month at market value.

Collecting and Investing in Antiques

Perhaps you have a talent for collecting and a love for antiques. Like other collectibles, they can be fun to own and they can turn into a very good investment over the years. They also have an immediate practical value. You can furnish your home today with reasonably good antiques for less than the cost of high-quality new furniture. The irony is that the new furniture will immediately depreciate and lose value, whereas antiques will usually retain and appreciate in value.

Antique shops, shows, and garage sales sometimes offer bargains. But if you are a budding collector, you may be better off spending most of your time at auctions. Auctions have three major advantages: (1) volume and variety, (2) no markups, and (3) usually more affordable prices.

Oriental Rugs

Another area you'll want to consider for both their investment potential and beauty is that of oriental rugs. You can rest assured that oriental rugs have reached the investment category when *The Financial Planner Magazine* devotes a large section with pictures in color to this investment media.

Oriental rugs come from one of the six schools considered oriental: (1) Persian (or Iranian), (2) Caucasian, (Turkoman, (4) Turkish, (5) Indian, or (6) Chinese. Valuable handcrafted carpets and rugs are named "oriental" because most of the great craftsmen down through history have operated east of Europe.

Rugs of investment quality are handmade and most are fifty years old. The price of a fine antique rug, with dimensions of four feet by six feet, from Turkey, Persia, or the Caucasus, can range from $2,000 to $10,000 or more. It is important for you to know what types of rugs come from which areas; for example, a Turkish village rug is coarser in weave than a Persian rug.

In appraising an oriental rug, experts take into account the following considerations:

1. Age

2. Condition (how are the edges and fringes, and is there any luster?)

3. Knot count (how many per square inch)

4. Tightness of weave (the tighter the weave the more valuable the rug)

5. Definition of pattern (the more definite a pattern, the more valuable the rug)

6. Singularity (How unique is the rug?)

7. Resale value of the rug (What price will the rug command upon resale or trade-in?)

Generally, the rug's resale value depends upon its overall quality as determined by the above criteria.

CONCLUSION

You may want to consider getting some of your assets out of the paper and into things, but I advise you to go very slowly when you move toward collectables.

At the end of the day, there's one simple fact that can't be denied – gold, silver and platinum are a beautiful and tangible asset, as well as the many other items that were discussed and there's nothing quite like holding the power of the future in your hands.

www.ingramcontent.com/pod-product-compliance
Lightning Source LLC
Chambersburg PA
CBHW081721220526
45468CB00008B/1936